Praise for *The Evolution of Education*

"*The Evolution of Education* is a provocative call to action on behalf of all students, whose future rests on our actions today. While the highlighted data paints a bleak picture of our current education system and its preparation of students, Bill Daggett offers hope through his poignant 'lessons for the future.' What we offer to our kids tells them what it is that we value. It is time to embrace the insights embedded within this book and transform our education system now to demonstrate that we value our kids' future."—Deb Delisle, CEO and president, the Alliance for Excellent Education, and former US assistant secretary of elementary and secondary education

"This is our chance to redefine and reimagine an education system that focuses first on our students, driven by a whole-child approach. To evolve means to do better, and we must. *The Evolution of Education* is a future-focused, sustainable framework responsive to adaptation, creativity, and innovation—all skills that our learners will need to thrive and be successful in their careers. This is a journey of excellence that is needed now more than ever!"—Deb Kerr, past president, AASA, and superintendent, Brown Deer School District, Brown Deer, Wisconsin

"*The Evolution of Education* provides a compelling and stark truth about a paradigm shift that is greatly needed in the education landscape. The reform ideologies presented by Dr. Daggett will improve our teaching and the learning ecosystem for all students. Using this book as a guidepost, practices and mindsets will collectively change to address the 'new' twenty-first-century economic demands."—Michael T. Conner, EdD, superintendent, Middletown Public Schools, Middletown, Connecticut

"The incremental pattern of schools looking back at previous-year test scores to determine how best to improve student performance is over! In this book, Dr. Daggett clearly lays out the many challenges we must overcome to create the future-focused schools our children and nation need. He then builds pathways lined with relationships, relevance, and rigor to get us there."—Raymond J. McNulty, president, Successful Practices Network, National Dropout Prevention Center

"Educational events must place learners in conditions that are unknown and uncomfortable, so that they can become creative designers of their future. Dr. Bill Daggett has again challenged thoughts about our schools' learning environments with a vision of the future, not that of our past."—Sam Houston, president and CEO, North Carolina Science, Mathematics, and Technology Education Center

"As an education leader and thought partner, Dr. Bill Daggett has always challenged me to think strategically about the existing education systems, structures, and methods of teaching and learning found within the K–12 public education sector. Without a doubt, *The Evolution of Education* not only extends that challenge but also calls on us to analyze our leadership efforts, and our efforts to ensure that the social, emotional, and mental well-being of our students, staff, and families are taken into consideration. I highly recommend this thoughtful resource, especially for those who are truly seeking to position their organization as a more future-focused system."—Andrew G. Houlihan, EdD, superintendent, Union County Public Schools, Monroe, North Carolina

"*The Evolution of Education* is a powerful call to action and a road map for how to fundamentally rethink how we educate our children. I recommend this book to any leader searching for a proven methodology to transform teaching and learning. It provides educators with the tools and knowledge necessary to support and advocate for sustainable school reform."—Michael Muñoz, superintendent, Rochester Public Schools, Rochester, Minnesota

The Evolution of Education

Preparing Students for Their Future (Not Our Past)

Willard R. Daggett, EdD

Foreword by Garth Harries

International Center for Leadership in Education®

International Center for Leadership in Education, Inc.
1587 Route 146
Rexford, New York 12148
www.LeaderEd.com
info@LeaderEd.com

ISBN: 978-1-328-03605-6

International Center For Leadership In Education
is a division of Houghton Mifflin Harcourt.

Printed in the United States of America.

5 6 7 8 9 10 0304 30 29 28 27 26 25 24 23

4500872045 ABCD

Contents

Acknowledgments

Although I'm listed as the sole author, writing a book takes a lot of help and encouragement. I owe a debt of gratitude to the many people who made this book possible. I'd like to offer a special thank you to all the wonderful people at the International Center for Leadership in Education (ICLE), but especially to Dr. Linda Lucey and Karen Wilkins. I'm honored to work with such a talented and dedicated group of professionals. I'd also like to thank the entire staff at Houghton Mifflin Harcourt (HMH), particularly Kate Gagnon, who did a masterful job guiding this book through the entire publishing process. Everyone at ICLE and HMH is committed to helping educators provide students with rigorous, relevant, future-focused instruction.

Valuable contributions were made to the book by Jeff Leeson of Benson-Collister, Julie Kendrick, Christine Utz, Jessica Goudeau, and Karen Propp. They helped in conceptualizing and creating the manuscript, offering many insights throughout the journey. Our production team champions, Susan Geraghty and Michele Jones, strived to ensure that this book is as polished and as timely as possible.

Several generous education and technology professionals allowed themselves to be interviewed for this book, including David Bain, Dr. Andrew Houlihan, Dr. Brad Breedlove, Katie Lyon, Tom Matson, Dr. Gary Hamilton, Jamie Bonczyk, Dr. Jean Desravines, Karen Cator, MaryEllen Elia, Ray McNulty, Dr. Rhoda Mhiripiri-Reed, Shauna McDonald, Samuel Houston, and many more. Not all interviewees made it into the book, but I'd like to express my gratitude for their helpful context and perspective.

Last, but certainly not least, I'd like to thank all the teachers and school and district administrators in the US and around the world. Often underappreciated, they work tirelessly to inspire, challenge, and care for our most treasured resource, our children.

About the Author

Willard Daggett, EdD, founding partner of the International Center for Leadership in Education (ICLE), is recognized worldwide for his proven ability to move preK–12 education systems toward more rigorous and relevant skills and knowledge for all students. For thirty years, he has crisscrossed our nation, as well as the industrialized world, to lead school reform efforts to effectively prepare students for their future.

An avid supporter of public education, he also challenges us to be more focused on our children's future than on maintaining the schools of our youth. His insights and leadership have caused nearly every major education association in the country, hundreds of school districts, numerous political and business leaders, publishers, and others to seek out his advice and guidance.

Before founding ICLE, Dr. Daggett was a teacher, local administrator, and a director with the New York State Education Department. Daggett is also the founder and chairman of the Successful Practices Network, which includes the National Dropout Prevention Center and the Career and Technical Education Technical Assistance Center.

He is the creator of the Rigor/Relevance Framework, which has recently become the cornerstone of much of the nation's school reform efforts. He is also the author of numerous books, textbooks, research reports, and journal articles about learning and education. Daggett has been recognized as a distinguished alumnus by both Temple University and the State University at Albany.

Daggett has a special commitment to individuals with disabilities. He and his wife, Bonnie, volunteer their time and lend their support to Wildwood Programs in upstate New York. Wildwood serves the needs of people of all ages who, like their daughter Audrey, have neurological impairments, learning disabilities, or autism, by enabling them to become the best that they can be.

About the International Center for Leadership in Education

The International Center for Leadership in Education (ICLE), a division of Houghton Mifflin Harcourt, challenges, inspires, and equips leaders and teachers to prepare their students for lifelong success. At the heart of all we do is the proven philosophy that the entire system must be aligned around instructional excellence—rooted in rigor, relevance, and relationships—to ensure that every student is prepared for a successful future.

Founded in 1991 by Dr. Bill Daggett, ICLE, through its team of thought leaders and consultants, helps schools and districts bring innovative practices to scale through professional learning opportunities and coaching partnerships guided by the cornerstones of our work: the Daggett System for Effective Instruction® and the Rigor/Relevance Framework®. In addition, ICLE shares successful practices that have a positive impact on student learning through keynote presentations; the Model Schools Conference, Leadership Academy, and other events; and a rich collection of publications. Learn more at LeaderEd.com.

Preface

THE NEW NORMAL

We're living through traumatic times. As we weather this difficult period, people all across the country ask me, When will we get back to normal? My answer is blunt: never. We'll never go back to the normal of 2019. Instead, there will be a new normal. This new normal will be deeply influenced by what we learn from the COVID-19 pandemic and the tragic—and unjust—deaths of African Americans through our criminal justice system.

For a moment, let's go back to a time before the COVID-19 crisis. When we go back, we realize that over the last several years, our emphasis on standards and state testing has shifted American education. To be clear: I'm not against standards or state testing. But our overwhelming responsibility to develop the academic skills of our students began to supersede everything else. Kindergarten teachers often lament that they used to spend time in structured play to teach social and emotional learning (SEL) skills through lessons on stopping and thinking, focusing, and having empathy for others. These are all skills students need throughout their K–12 school careers—and beyond. But because of our heavy emphasis on getting kids ready for the next test or the next grade, we began earlier and earlier to drive academics into education. When this happened, something had to give. We didn't lengthen the school day or stretch the school year, so we started to lose these broader SEL skills.

Next, let's revisit the death of George Floyd on May 25, 2020. After this tragic event, the structural inequities in this country became clear to all of us. Many of us already understood these inequities—inequities that Black and Indigenous people, and people of color have lived with for centuries—yet we failed to address them. As we've thought more about inequity, we've realized that it can't be addressed just at the national level. Schools must play a role in correcting inequity. Each and every one of us as individuals must play a role in correcting inequity. As we reopen schools, as we consider the future of our children—of all children—I want you to pause and reflect. I want you to ask yourself, *Can I as an individual take action to increase equity?* And together as a school or school district, can we take action to address the structural inequities that have plagued us for centuries?

Even before these events, we were already experiencing an alarming spike in mental health issues affecting our children. This rise is discussed in detail in chapter 1 of this book. But very briefly, as advanced technology took over, federal, state, and local policymakers began to focus more on academics—which, in turn, led to more issues with mental health and well-being. Then the pandemic hit, and many educators and education leaders discovered that they had to rethink their priorities. As schools across the country closed, the primary concern of educators became feeding all the children who face poverty and food scarcity.

Poverty—along with a host of other problems, such as homelessness and abuse—is a growing issue in this country. Understandably, these types of issues produce trauma. In many cases, these sorts of traumas speak directly to our problems with systemic inequity. In other cases, trauma comes from bullying, violence, feelings of loneliness, or other social factors. This trauma rarely starts in school, but rather is usually centered in the home—or the lack of a home. In fact, school may be the one place where many students can escape trauma. So what happened when we shuttered schools and sent students home? We placed them in a traumatic environment all day, every day. Beyond this, recent events have added to many students' feelings of loneliness and anxiety. Before 2020, it was estimated that nearly two-thirds of students faced some sort of trauma in their lives.[1] Now, after COVID-19 and our recent social unrest, it's safe to say that nearly all students have faced some degree of trauma. Extended school closures have led to exponential growth of mental health issues in students.

This rise in mental health issues has led many educators to realize that in our drive to increase academic performance, we've lost sight of our single most important responsibility: caring for the whole child.

With students back in school, the new normal is about the whole child. It's about developing and supporting the whole child. This affects staffing, evaluation, and implementation in schools. It affects how we use the support staff in our schools. This new normal also includes changes in how we use technology to augment learning and increase equity. Pre-crisis, in school district after school district, we tried to make twenty-first-century technology conform to our twentieth-century schools. We've now learned that we need to transform our twentieth-century schools to conform to the reality of our twenty-first-century technology. Although this new paradigm includes remote learning, it doesn't demand a complete shift to digital or online learning. More so now than ever, we all understand the importance of teachers and classrooms. Teachers create relevance and foster relationships; classrooms support a culture of rigor and inclusion. Instead, this change means redefining the roles of teachers, as well as of parents and the community. The crisis has helped us understand that we need to use technology to support all students in reaching their potential. For this transformation to occur, teachers, administrators, and parents need to be supported through professional development and other support systems.

This has been a difficult year. Overall, however, I have tremendous hope. As tragedies often do, our current situation has crystallized many issues, ranging from education to public health to environmental degradation. I believe we'll begin to take a harder look at many of these issues and work toward greater investment in science. We'll work together to share knowledge, raise community awareness, and support local industries. We'll nourish kindness and a spirit of togetherness. I believe we must lean into this hope; we must encourage one another to find our inner strength and express our deepest humanity.

But I also have a fear.

My fear is that when we look at this new normal, we'll get stuck in 2020 and the lessons of the moment. We'll focus so intently on the pandemic, the social unrest, and the school closures of this year that we'll lose sight of 2021, 2022, and 2023. Those who have heard me speak know that I stress the importance of being future focused. Even when the present is difficult, we need to put a stake in the ground three to five years out and build back from the future. Throughout this book, I discuss emerging technologies such as automation, augmented intelligence, and artificial intelligence. These technologies will have a profound impact on the skills our children need to succeed at work, at home, and in their communities. As tempting as it is to get fixated on the present, the new normal cannot be based on 2020. Instead, it must be based on 2025, or even 2030. We must be future focused as we address the whole child and as we assimilate new technology. If we as school leaders are to participate in the evolution of education, we must push past today and look beyond tomorrow—we must embrace the future.

Bill Daggett
November 2020

Foreword

A few days after Bill Daggett announced his intention to retire from the International Center for Leadership in Education (ICLE), he and I swapped early morning photos of the sun coming up for each of us: he from his home on Cape Cod, I from my family's organic farm in Connecticut. "Every dawn is a new tomorrow," we wrote to each other.

Bill has spent his career looking to the new tomorrow for education. Houghton Mifflin Harcourt's CEO Jack Lynch describes Bill as a futurist with an uncanny gift for looking over the horizon and using his surprising expertise in robotics, nanotechnology, and artificial intelligence to describe what he sees. This book shares that gift, providing page after page of insights into the ways our technology, economy, and society have changed, and will continue to change, and exploring the implications of those changes for our schools and the students who must thrive in that new tomorrow.

Another of Bill's gifts is to respect and honor the place where we are standing right now and the people he is standing with. Spend any time with Bill, and you will recognize his straightforward joy in what surrounds him, particularly the people surrounding him. Professionally, that translates into a profound respect for educators and the work they do every day. Bill doesn't describe the future of education to tell us we aren't good enough or even to tell us we aren't doing the right thing. He describes the future in order to unleash the great power of educators, to inspire and help us all to make the changes we need and want.

I have been privileged to lead deep systemic change in two school districts: New York City and New Haven, Connecticut. In reflecting on those efforts—and all the successes and failures I experienced during the journey—the essential wisdom of Bill's approach to school transformation becomes even more apparent. A clear vision is both inspiring and orienting. Inspiring, because it describes a future that educators and families want to move toward. Orienting, because it gives educators a way to focus together so that they can make a thousand daily decisions and interact in ways that point in the same coordinated direction. Honesty about the problems of the current system without casting blame or fault allows for collaboration—we all work through the features of today that need to be changed in the move to tomorrow. And identifying the tip of the spear—whether that is small schools, teacher professionalism, or data teams—means identifying straightforward steps to take that can begin to create transformation for students. In my experience, the only way systems improve is through that mix of vision, no-fault problem-solving, and concrete and collective progress. We must have revolutionary goals and an evolutionary path to achieve them.

This vision of ambitious but unifying and practical change is particularly important during this moment of history. The sudden school closures and subsequent remote learning for US schoolchildren exposed the deep shortcomings of our conventional approach to instruction and our implicit acceptance of social and technological inequities that affect learning. And the acceleration of Black Lives Matter and other social movements highlight how profoundly disconnected and unseen so many of our citizens and students feel. These realities challenge our current educational systems and strain the normal ways teaching and learning happen in this country.

One reaction to this moment would be to focus on the here and now: the immediate plans for safety and security, the ordering of materials, supplies, and social justice curricula. Another would be to abandon the existing systems entirely, to move students into even more isolated communities and even less relevant and relationship-based instruction. Bill's full gift, and the orientation of ICLE, is to respect simultaneously the situation we are in right now and the future we want to build. For educators, that means addressing the unique demands that arise during a global pandemic and taking actions in ways that look to our future so we can move in that direction. It means planning more project-based and engaging lessons (Quad D), which can be used face-to-face or virtually, creating and sharing videos that give students an identity and presence in their classrooms, and implementing a thousand other ideas that reflect the truths of rigor, relevance, and relationship as applied to the future we are building together.

As I write this, Bill is moving into his new proverbial day, planning to spend less time at ICLE and more time with his family and on new projects. He leaves all of us in education and ICLE with immense gifts. Please know that we at ICLE will keep doing what Bill has always done and will continue to do: focus on the future and use that future to inspire evolution today.

If all of us in education can focus on the future and take action dawn after dawn, day after day, we will give ALL students the education, the opportunity, and the future they rightly deserve. And, ultimately, this will be the fullest celebration of Bill's legacy.

Garth Harries
Managing partner, ICLE

Introduction

There is an employment epidemic in America right now: today's students are unprepared to succeed in the workforce. According to a recent survey by the National Association of Colleges and Employers of over four thousand recent college graduates and two hundred employers, only about 50 percent of employers considered students proficient in such areas as oral and written communication, critical thinking, problem solving, and leadership.[1] Similarly, LinkedIn recently published its annual Top Skills list, which analyzes data across the professional social network in order to rank which skills are both in high demand *and* in low supply. The top five? Creativity, persuasion, collaboration, adaptability, and time management.[2]

I hear the same concerns expressed by private sector executives at events such as the Business Roundtable Innovation Summit. They hire employees who look good on paper, but often lack the most critical capabilities needed in today's workplace—the ability to manage a project, the capacity to collaborate with colleagues, and even a basic understanding of how to contribute to a meeting.

The most alarming part of this trend? These skills will only become more important as technology continues to transform the labor market. According to the World Economic Forum, in a report called *The Future of Jobs*, the top ten skills needed to thrive at work in 2020 and beyond include complex problem solving, critical thinking, creativity, people management, coordinating with others, emotional intelligence, active listening, service operation, negotiation, and cognitive flexibility.[3]

This means that all students must be empowered with more than technical expertise or academic achievement to build a strong workforce and a prosperous society. They must develop into "Renaissance" individuals in a technological age. They must be adaptable, able to solve problems, and able to collaborate effectively.

Instead of actively building these types of skills, however, too many of us in education have worked to incrementally improve a system that focuses on showing up, following rules, and memorizing facts—the same sorts of skills required for jobs that employers can easily automate. Too often, our schools revert to the methods of the past to teach students the skills they need for tomorrow. And frankly, far too many of us think our job is simply to get kids ready for the next test, the next grade, or the next level of education. This is a strategy that prepares them for our past—not their future.

In short, as we enter the third decade of the twenty-first century, our education system hasn't changed fast enough from its nineteenth-century form. The rate of innovation in schools and curricula hasn't kept up with our economic, technological, and societal progress. Memorization and simple comprehension no longer work. We see too many students who find schooling meaningless. Even high achievers are often just playing the game and are not deeply engaged by schoolwork. Consequently, confidence in our K–12 education system is eroding because we're not preparing our students for the world they'll inherit and the challenges they'll need to meet.

The real victims in all of this? The young people in classrooms around the country who will find it harder than ever to establish a career, create a home, and build a future. If we continue to teach students with our current model, issues with employment and equity will get worse and more widespread. Graduates prepared for the older way of working will fail to find careers that allow them to become self-sufficient or lead satisfying lives.

If this message doesn't resonate with you, just take a moment to think about all the parents you know with a daughter or son in her or his teens or early twenties. How many of those parents are anxious—often to the point of panic—about their child developing into an independent adult? And how about the young adults you know? How many are four-year-college graduates who now live at home or still need financial help from their parents? According to Pew Research Center analysis, today's young adults between the ages of eighteen and thirty-four are less likely to be living independently of their families today than at any other period in the last 120 years, including during the depths of the Great Depression.[4] And according to another recent survey, over half of parents are sacrificing their retirement savings in order to help their grown children pay rent, cell phone bills, and credit card bills.[5]

And these are our *success stories*. These are the model students: the high achievers and curve setters, the college graduates and graduate students. When our best and our brightest, our success stories, are coming home in unparalleled numbers, it should be a wake-up call for all of us.

It's nothing short of a potential for social and economic disaster.

A Reason for Optimism

This situation sounds dire, right? But be assured, there is hope. I believe our public education system is the best in the world, period. I don't say this just as a lifelong educator; I say it also as a parent and grandparent. Do we have the highest standards? No. Do we have the most relevant standards? We don't. How can I say we have the best schools if we don't have the highest or most relevant standards? I can say it for one simple reason: in the United States, we educate all children. It's our commitment to equity and excellence that makes our schools the best.

Consider the sheer scope of our nearly two-hundred-year-old US system of education. We now teach up to seventy-four million students a year. Our system is one of the most ambitious collective projects in our country's history. With a few possible exceptions, no other public or private institution has proven so successful at such a large scale over such a long period of time. For all the hype, Google has existed for just over twenty years, and Facebook is even younger. Apple has been around for four decades and has reached millions of consumers, but even its successes pale in comparison. Our system of education—and the many professionals who support it—has kept the United States at the forefront of the global economy for generations. It has alleviated poverty and addressed inequities; it has provided hope and nurtured potential. It has helped hundreds of millions of people live higher-quality lives, raise families, and contribute to the betterment of society. And, of course, it has delivered some of the greatest breakthroughs and innovations that humankind has ever known, including the eradication of deadly diseases, the development of life-changing technologies, and the exploration of outer space.

So let's put aside the idea that education in the US is "broken" or that administrators and teachers are "failing." The world has been changing at the speed of Moore's law, and technology continues to alter the workplace at an unprecedented rate, but many of our basic principles and instructional practices still work. We do need to change our approach to providing students with the support and skills necessary to succeed in the future, but not by scrapping the system or denigrating its many thoughtful, caring professionals. American schools are remarkable places, capable of delivering excitement, beauty, and enlightenment on a daily basis, but it's my belief that we in education have collectively taken our eye off the ultimate objective—making students independent. Our K–12 schools don't need a radical overhaul; they just need a strong nudge toward a new vision for twenty-first century learning.

Evolution—Not Revolution

I have a favorite saying that I use in many of my presentations: "Education needs to be evolutionary, not revolutionary. Revolutionaries get killed." Throughout the last few decades, we've had many school reform "revolutionaries" who have tried to completely reinvent school. In their enthusiasm to disrupt K–12 education, these smart, well-funded, and well-meaning idealists have failed to consider the norms of schooling that have developed over centuries of educational practice. They've underestimated the strong social beliefs of educators, parents, voters, and taxpayers about what school looks like and how it operates. In doing so, they've doomed school reform to a cycle of overly ambitious reinvention, middling results, and inevitable regression.

As these well-intentioned people debate one another, we've doubled down on standardized testing, enacting programs of false accountability and anchoring our students to outdated models of education that fail to teach the skills needed in today's economy. While technological breakthroughs speed ahead, education continues to rely too much on a dated concept of proficiency and too little on science-based tools such as data analytics.

Yes, our schools need to evolve. But what if, rather than trying to dismantle the current system and build a new one, we put the same energy into proven programs that can prosper within mainstream public schools? What if teachers could incorporate new, more effective and engaging modes of classroom interaction without having to discard everything they've learned

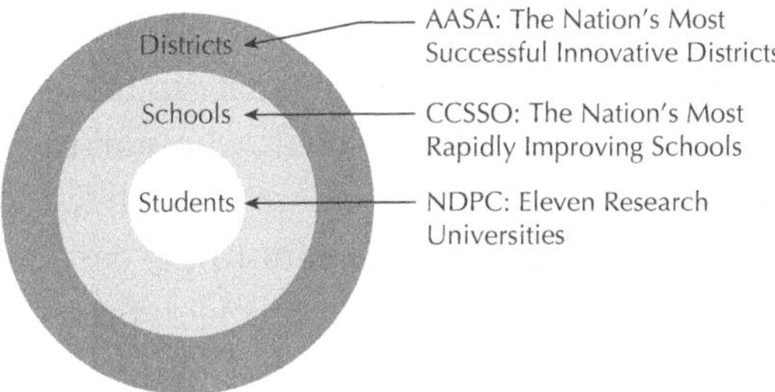

FIGURE I.1 Three National Studies

and done in the past? Sounds almost too good to be true. In *The Evolution of Education*, I provide a sustainable framework for developing the success skills that enable students to work, grow, and thrive both today and in the future.

Recently, I've had the privilege of chairing multiple national commissions that have closely studied the characteristics of the nation's most rapidly improving schools at three different levels: the district level, the school level, and the student level. Figure I.1 shows how these studies fit together to offer a comprehensive picture of needed change in education.

The first study—sponsored by the American Association of School Superintendents (AASA)—focused on the nation's most successful innovative districts. In this case, we picked twenty-five districts out of sixteen thousand nationwide to analyze what they did differently to improve student performance. This work built off of an earlier national study I chaired for the Council of Chief State Officers (CCSO) that looked at the nation's most rapidly improving schools. Because you can have a great school in a bad district, this study focused on what principals, teachers, and staff were doing within their individual buildings to increase success. Finally, I chaired a study for the National Dropout Prevention Center, in association with eleven research universities, that identified the best practices for educating our most vulnerable students. Combined, these three studies provide a clear picture of how our schools—big and small, and at all levels—can better prepare students for an uncertain future.

And make no mistake: we must prepare today's students not for a single career but for lifelong learning and collaboration as workers and citizens. Building these skills is critical for our future prosperity, given estimates that roughly half the children in kindergarten today will work in jobs that don't yet exist. In addition, they'll be dealing with societal problems we can barely begin to imagine. Therefore, we need to change our approach to educating students, and we need to do it in a way that capitalizes on the strengths of our current schools and the professionals who staff them. Applying the strategies outlined throughout this book, we can pull K–12 education into the twenty-first century, making it relevant to the current world and the future workplace. But like all important changes, these won't happen on their own—they're driven by leaders.

All Leaders, All Levels

As both a practical and research-based resource, *The Evolution of Education* is tailored to a broad group of education leaders that includes principals, vice principals, superintendents, assistant superintendents, and other administrators. Today, education leaders have an almost overwhelming range of responsibilities, such as school safety, whole-child growth, mental wellness, relationship development, and academic accountability. Throughout this book, I offer strategies for addressing all of these responsibilities, and many more. And because true school leadership takes place at all levels, from the district office to school hallways and playing fields, the book is equally helpful to teacher leaders, instructional coaches, professional developers, counselors, and professional learning practitioners. The framework I provide can be readily embraced and employed by educators at every grade level and in every type of school, transforming mundane classrooms into rich educational environments that ensure the development of future-proof skills.

Beyond education professionals, *The Evolution of Education* is likely to be the book that school administrators recommend to new school board members, PTA members, and deeply involved parents who want to better understand the changes needed to improve education. The simple reality is informed parents and concerned citizens are the key to any true education reform. Offering a clear-eyed picture of both the current and future states of K–12 education, this book gives these readers the tools and knowledge necessary to support and advocate for sustainable school reform.

The What, Why, and How

To reach each of these audiences, *The Evolution of Education* addresses the current challenges in many districts and offers research-based solutions to these challenges. Along the way, I debunk a few myths about students and educators, explore developing trends and new technologies, and explain what these changes mean for our profession. I start in chapter 1 by providing an overview of the difficulties—from anxiety to bullying to homelessness—faced by today's students. Chapter 2 then takes a sober look at the future, focusing on technological developments, changing demographics, and evolving job requirements. Chapter 3 explains how best to address the previously discussed behavioral health issues and changing job market through social and emotional learning (SEL). The chapter includes specific tools for implementing SEL initiatives in schools and classrooms. Chapter 4 follows with a look at the importance of creating relationships in schools, especially to help drive rigor and relevance. Next, chapter 5 explores the concept of being future focused rather than forward focused, and provides ways to prepare students for an uncertain, more competitive economy. Chapter 6 focuses on the weaknesses of our current proficiency model—one driven by standardized testing—and explains the importance of growth, especially as it relates to lifelong learning. In chapter 7, I take an in-depth look at data, its strengths, its limitations, and its future in improving educational outcomes. Finally, chapter 8 culminates with an examination of what all these trends, changes, and new technologies mean in the context of the classroom.

To help readers incorporate and reference many of the ideas throughout the book, I've included key Lessons for the Future and salient messages from experts in each chapter. To discover additional resources or read updates, please see www.leadered.com/evolution-of-education.

Technology has radically transformed both the workplace and the abilities required to compete for a job. Employers across all types of industries increasingly require a more advanced, application-centered skill set, and nowhere has this disruption hit harder than in the types of middle-wage jobs for which our public education system used to prepare students. Automation started to make many occupations obsolete decades ago, as robots replaced factory workers and personal computers took over most rote office tasks.

These challenges are only going to get more difficult.

With the emergence of powerful new technologies—artificial intelligence, robotics, computer-to-brain interfacing, and genetic engineering, among others—machines will begin to replace humans in performing not only physical tasks but also more cognitive, "human" tasks. A public debate has emerged about the number of jobs threatened by AI and similar technologies, but what's clear is that portions of every occupation will change.

The key purpose of education—at least to my way of thinking—is to prepare students for this increasingly unpredictable future. Therefore, ask yourself: Have you and your colleagues begun to take the bold steps forward to instruct students for the twenty-first century? And if you haven't yet, why not? What are you waiting for? For things to get worse?

You've picked up this book, which means you've taken the first big step forward. The call to change our schools is urgent. It's as urgent as it has ever been. The pace of change in our world is only increasing. The longer we take to get started, the harder the work becomes for all of us—administrators, teachers, counselors, and parents alike. So let's dive in now, before our problems become more difficult, the costs greater, and the stakes higher. We owe it to the next generation of employees and employers; to the coming parents, homeowners, and problem solvers; to the future innovators, entrepreneurs, and community leaders.

We owe it to the students of today, who will become the citizens of tomorrow.

1

Kids Today

Sixteen-year-old Cameron Lee was popular, athletic, and an excellent student. A junior at Gunn High School in Palo Alto, California—a district in Silicon Valley known for its high-performing schools—Cameron often bragged to his friends about staying up all night to study. He played basketball, pulled pranks on other students, and earned all A's in his classes. By all appearances, he was a normal, well-adjusted kid on the fast track to success.

But then Cameron took his own life. Depressed, anxious, and exhausted, he stepped in front of a southbound commuter train.

The local community was devastated. Cameron hadn't displayed the typical warning signs of an at-risk teen, but he also wasn't the first Palo Alto student to take his or her own life. In recent years, six students had committed suicide. Five of these students put themselves in front of an oncoming train.

Why are so many teens committing suicide? And why is this happening even with students who are high achievers and seemingly well adjusted?

Today, students are facing a serious mental health crisis. In the last few years, we've seen skyrocketing rates of anxiety, depression, loneliness, self-harm, and suicide in our youth. Over a ten-year period from 2007 to 2017, the suicide rates for Americans ages ten to twenty-four increased by 56 percent. And according to the Centers for Disease Control and Prevention (CDC), mental health and behavioral disorders are diagnosed in one out of six kids ages two to eight, and most commonly in non-Hispanic white boys. Approximately four million kids ages three to seventeen have been diagnosed with anxiety, and nearly two million suffer from depression. Behavioral disorders have also increased, with more than one in three children displaying problematic behavior.[1]

Many of these numbers are worse for girls. According to the World Health Organization (WHO), 21 percent of female students ages thirteen to eighteen suffer a serious mental health condition during their developmental years. The incidence of depression and suicide among girls has gone up at a truly alarming rate. Since 2010, among teen girls,[2]

- Suicide rates increased 65 percent.
- Severe depression increased 58 percent.
- Feelings of hopelessness increased 12 percent.

Suicide is but one of the heartbreaking manifestations of the serious crisis we're facing in schools and throughout society. Students are not only taking their own lives more often but also thinking about suicide more than in previous years. According to the CDC, 17 percent of high school students and 8 percent of college students have thought seriously about suicide. Suicidal ideation is even occurring among students as young as nine or ten. Suicide is now the second leading cause of death among young people, surpassed only by accidents.[3] As we saw with the story of Cameron Lee, suicide is a risk for all our students, even the ones who appear to be happy, well supported, and successful.

This should be—no, *needs to be*—a wake-up call for all of us. Our children are facing a mental health crisis so severe that education professionals can no longer downplay it or ignore it. And it shouldn't take a tragic event like a suicide to see the broader signs of the struggles that today's students are facing and, all too often, failing to overcome.

A Generation in Trouble

Many of us have noticed the drastic increase in the numbers of anxious and overwhelmed students in our classrooms. The National Institute of Mental Health reports that anxiety is the most common mental health disorder in the United States, with nearly one in three adolescents affected by it. There are plenty of legitimate reasons to feel anxious in our world today. Some students are raised in abusive families or live in neighborhoods plagued by violence, or they're experiencing food insecurity or homelessness. But students aren't just worried about their lives outside school. One high school student in North Carolina worried that if he didn't do well on a quiz at school, "then I'll get a bad grade in the class, I won't get into the college I want, I won't get a good job, and I'll be a total failure." A 2018 Pew poll of adolescents ages thirteen to seventeen reported that nine out of ten students believe they *must* do well in school. The same study also found that 70 percent of participants believed that anxiety and depression were a serious concern for their peers.[4]

Clinical depression is also rising at an alarming rate. According to WHO, depression is the single most prevalent cause of illness and disability in adolescents worldwide. Data reported by health insurance provider Blue Cross Blue Shield showed a 63 percent increase in children ages twelve to seventeen being diagnosed with major depression in 2016. While the rates have been steadily increasing among teenagers, depression is also more prevalent among our youngest learners. Children as young as three years old are now at a higher risk for suffering from depression, especially if they have other mental health and behavioral concerns, such as anxiety or ADHD. Further, students dealing with an episode of depression aren't always receiving the critical help they need, which magnifies this problem. Only 33 percent of boys sought treatment, compared to 45 percent of teenage girls.[5] These rates of anxiety and depression have deep roots in other social trends, such as loneliness and self-harm, that have accelerated over the last couple of decades.

The Loneliest Generation

The current generation of children growing up today is on track to be one of the loneliest on record. According to the results of an extensive 2020 study, 62 percent of people under twenty-four years of age say they feel lonely at least once a week.[6] Despite being members of the most connected and tech-literate generations, adolescents today feel more isolated than before and lack meaningful relationships in their lives. The truth is, all those hours of screen time don't translate to deeper connections with their peers. In fact, teens who spend time on their smartphones and social media are more likely to report mental health issues compared to teens who spend their time face-to-face with friends, exercising, or reading a physical book.

The effects of loneliness are more dangerous than they might appear. Douglas Nemecek, chief medical officer for behavioral health at Cigna, emphasizes the link between loneliness and preexisting conditions, such as anxiety and depression. "Research has found that loneliness has the same impact on mortality as smoking 15 cigarettes a day, making it even more dangerous than obesity," said Nemecek. On top of that, loneliness has been linked to deadly maladies such as heart disease and stroke.[7]

Overworked, Exhausted, and Terrified of Failure

Even in the presence of good schools and ample opportunity, many of our students have been pushed to the point of exhaustion. In part, this is because the stakes are higher than ever before. Many parents and teachers today are obsessed with test scores and making sure their children get accepted into elite colleges. Understandably, this has come to be seen as the route to future success and happiness in life. And what parent doesn't want his or her children to be happy and successful? But the average student now takes more aptitude tests than ever before. During the 2016–17 school year, more than 6.7 million test takers completed the SAT or a PSAT-related assessment.[8] The increased focus on testing means that students spend more time studying, which overloads their already busy schedules. In hopes of standing out in a highly competitive college applicant pool, they must also dedicate hours of practice to sports, music, or other extracurricular activities. These used to be seen as fun or life enriching, but now for some students they're approached as application or resume builders.

Even for students with an impressive academic record and stellar test scores, admittance to one of the top colleges is far from guaranteed. Colleges have been steadily decreasing their acceptance rates, which means that students and parents feel the need to double down on studying and testing to compete for fewer spots. The pressure for early achievement has damaging effects on our children's physical and mental well-being. Stanford psychology professor Carol Dweck, author of the best-selling book *Mindset: The New Psychology of Success*, observed that "kids seem more exhausted and brittle today. I'm getting much more fear of failure, fear of evaluation, than I've gotten before."[9] This fear of failure is crippling for young people. It prevents them from taking risks, struggling with a problem, or learning from their mistakes.

In essence, it prevents them from growing up.

An Epidemic of Self-Harm

Most of our students enduring a mental health crisis aren't equipped to handle the experience on their own and therefore often turn to destructive coping behaviors, such as self-harm. As many as one in twelve high school students has deliberately harmed himself or herself, by cutting, burning, or other self-destructive practices. Most self-harmers begin at age fifteen; the behavior lasts for five years or more. The practice is more common among female students, though the statistics are high for males as well: one in four girls deliberately harms herself, compared to one in ten boys.[10] Research shows that the behavior tends to decline with age, but clearly, our students need more help and more adaptive strategies for addressing their pain and trauma.

EXPERT IM

In 2010 when I was a principal in Houston ISD, I cannot recall a single elementary child ever being referred to a counselor or to me who had a suicidal ideation. Last year, in Union County, our leading suicide referrals were in grades 4 and 5. That says a lot to me as an educator. When it comes to kids who are in crisis, it's not discriminatory.

—Dr. Andrew G. Houlihan
Superintendent of Union County School District in North Carolina

According to the Anxiety and Depression Association of America, 25 percent of these types of cases of anxiety or depression occur by age fourteen.[11] Compound this with a crippling fear of failure, isolation from family and friends, and increased rates of self-harm and suicide, and we're facing a waking nightmare for students, educators, and parents alike. This raises an important question for all of us: What's causing this unprecedented growth in mental and behavioral health issues?

The Dark Side of Technology

New technologies have transformed how we live, work, and interact. Think about how many tools the smartphone has replaced in your life. You use it to access your calendar, as an alarm clock, to keep your schedule, and to forecast the weather. It has replaced your camera, shopping cart, and newspaper. It's also home to social media apps like Instagram, Snapchat, and YouTube. Today's students have never known a world without access to all these capabilities and platforms. Smartphones are an extension of their world, and most of them are more comfortable online than hanging out with friends or going to a party.

This is a big part of the problem.

Technology is making our kids lonelier and more at risk for mental health disorders, a problem discussed earlier in the chapter.[12] It can also be damaging to their reputation and performance at school. The constant use of technology has created an expectation of immediate feedback. For instance, a child can post a photo to Instagram or share a video on TikTok and instantly receive "likes" and comments. This rapid-fire format means that a post can quickly go viral and appear before the eyes of millions of people across the globe. Even if the audience is just a child's peers, the desire for instant gratification is addictive, and reinforces behaviors that don't translate well in the physical world. Faster technology equates to less patience and decreased focus.

The internet and today's ubiquitous social media have changed how children think, encouraging them to scan information quickly and make hasty decisions about the content. In a study conducted by researchers at the University of Massachusetts Amherst, the majority of participants said they would abandon a video if it took more than two seconds to load.[13] Most internet users read only 20 percent of the text on a website. Lacking important skills such as attentiveness and the ability to delay gratification, students are more likely to feel frustrated when feedback isn't immediate—especially if it isn't explicitly positive. Over time, these patterns are damaging to students' health, resilience, and ability to concentrate.

Although our children are developing relationships through social media apps, such relationships are not the kinds of deep, personal connections needed for good behavioral health. Kids may have hundreds or even thousands of online "friends," and they may spend hours on their phone exchanging videos and texts, but these interactions rarely qualify as meaningful. To be clear: I'm not arguing for the banning of smartphones or tablets; I'm not a Luddite who wants to turn back the clock to typewriters and snail mail. Social media can be an important platform for interactions among children. It allows them to remain in contact with one another, to offer support and stay up to date on their friends' lives.

But—and this is an important but—the pervasiveness of digital interactions as compared to face-to-face encounters can have damaging long-term effects. It encourages kids to be inauthentic, favoring curated content over their actual experiences. They feel pressured to create a social media persona that presents their best, most attractive self because that's what earns them the attention and adulation they crave. This means that exchanges on social media are less genuine than they are in real life. How can children form a meaningful connection with someone if they aren't allowed to be themselves? How can they discover who they are if they're not allowed to explore and express their true selves?

Even worse, technology has also created new opportunities for threatening behavior. Cyberbullying is now a common occurrence, with 32 percent of teenagers reporting that they've been harassed online.[14] Students complain that content is shared without their consent, their communications are rarely considered private, and rumors spread faster than ever before. As we've all seen or experienced, the internet is a great place to stir up drama. More than half of teens have witnessed their peers start a conflict on social media, and over a quarter of them have gotten into a fight with a friend over something that occurred online.[15]

When the drama escalates, kids have a litany of new tools for ostracizing their soon-to-be-ex-friends. They unfriend them, unfollow them, delete their photos, or even block them from seeing their own content. In today's world, being digitally banished by your peers can be just as hurtful as a face-to-face dismissal. In some cases, it can even be more harmful, because the degree of separation created by technology removes important ingredients of human interaction such as empathy or accountability. Everyone knows it's easier to lash out or hurt someone using a keyboard than in a face-to-face confrontation.

We as adults, as educators and instructors, need to ask ourselves whether social media platforms really have children's best interest in mind. The short answer: no.

As Facebook, YouTube, Twitter, and other media companies scramble to respond to the backlash against a lack of privacy and filtering, our children are increasingly being exposed to troubling content. Even a simple internet search can lead to explicit images or websites that kids are not yet emotionally capable of dealing with. Experts have advised parents to limit screen time and install filters on all devices, but these approaches rarely shield children from possible threats. And in truth, most kids know or find a way to get around these types of blocks and filters.

This isn't just a problem for teenagers. Children as young as eight or nine are stumbling on sexually explicit material while playing games, using apps, or watching videos.[16] More and more, violent acts are streamed on social media for anyone to see. According to the American Academy of Pediatrics, frequent exposure to violence desensitizes children and encourages them to view violence as a suitable option. Even though many schools have already implemented digital literacy courses in their curriculum, it bears repeating that our students are particularly vulnerable to misinformation, fake news, and controversial content.

These problems aren't just developing in a virtual world or through social media platforms. Many of them are being exacerbated by changes in our concrete, real-world environment.

Changes at Home

Technology isn't the only thing that's changing our students. Shifting home lives and a new wave of parenting styles are impacting their emotional and cognitive development. Why is it that so many of our students lack critical skills—independence, self-reliance, determination, and the like? Well, many of them are being lovingly smothered by well-intentioned parents.

Today's Hovering, Pushy Parents

Some parents are a little *too* invested in their kids' lives. At this end of the spectrum are so-called helicopter and snowplow parents, the former vigilantly hovering over their children to protect them from negative experiences, and the latter clearing the path of all obstacles so that their child never has to struggle. Of course, these types of parents have good intentions: they want to shield their child from failure and frustration, from painful experiences and trauma. But at the same time, they end up stunting their child's growth. The children of snowplow parents, in particular, are completely dependent on adults to make doctor's appointments, to handle conflicts with friends and roommates, and to remind them to wake up for school or hand in an assignment. What will these students do when they enter the workforce? More important: What will these students do when their future bosses criticize their work or effort?

Spoiler alert: their parents will call their bosses, complain, and vouch for them. Mom and Dad to the rescue! Again.

As a part of this trend, children's schedules are now carefully monitored and controlled by the adults in their lives. Remember being able to run around the neighborhood with a pack of other kids, playing until the sun went down and you were called home for dinner? This kind of idyllic, pre-internet childhood is a rare phenomenon today. Many parents, influenced by real and perceived dangers, constantly keep their kids in sight. Factor in school, screen time, and extracurricular activities, and it's no wonder our kids feel as though they don't have a moment to explore and understand the world on their own terms.

The amount of time children spend playing has been cut in half, compared to their parents' generation. As one gym teacher reported, some of his students don't know how to play simple games like four square, jump rope, or kickball. American kids spend 90 percent of their free time at home in front of a screen, watching TV, or playing video games, according to a study by researchers at UCLA.[17] Even when kids are physically active, they're still closely supervised—and often coached and critiqued—by adults. This is in spite of the fact that children learn to refine higher-functioning skills such as resourcefulness, teamwork, and leadership through open-ended forms of play. As Jamie Bonczyk, executive director at Hopkins Early Learning Center, told me, " Free play is the number one generator of neural circuits for young kids."

EXPERT IM

Play is a universal human behavior. In fact, all mammals play. Play is how we come to understand the ever-changing world around us, as well as a way in which we come to understand ourselves. We take risks and we learn the skills that we need to be successful in a community, including problem solving and collaboration.

—Shauna McDonald
Executive director, Playworks Minnesota

The simple truth is, children need to spend time with other children. And they need to do so without an adult constantly intervening. If parents always jump in to handle conflicts or setbacks, kids never learn to resolve disputes or bounce back on their own. They fail to develop a sense of autonomy, and as a result these kids are more anxious, self-conscious, and likely to be diagnosed with anxiety or depression. They're also less flexible and have difficulty coping with stressful situations.

But what about the opposite end of the spectrum? What if parents aren't around at all?

Absentee Parents and Disrupted Homes

Increasing numbers of American children have little adult contact in the home. Whether these kids are living in a single-parent household or with parents who both work all the time, the absence of these important family figures is significant. Furthermore, some of these children are missing one or both of their parents due to incarceration. The American prison population has grown exponentially since 1980, with the number of incarcerated women increasing by a mind-boggling 750 percent. As a result, at least five million children currently have or have had a parent behind bars.[18] This kind of separation has devastating effects. Kids who grow up without a mother or father at home are more likely to suffer from depression, anxiety, and behavioral problems. They have higher dropout rates, are more likely to use drugs, and experience more isolation as adults. They're also more likely to enter the criminal justice system themselves, perpetuating many of these issues for generations to come.

Although our economy has improved since the Great Recession, the number of homeless children in our schools has actually increased to more than 1.3 million.[19] This means that an alarming number of students we educators encounter each day are in acute crisis. Explored extensively in professor Tyrone Howard's book *All Students Must Thrive*, housing insecurity and homelessness trigger unique stressors, including disruption of a family's routine, additional scrutiny and surveillance, and increased fear of a child being taken and placed into foster care. Over the last decade, we've also seen an increase in the number of families "doubled-up" in apartments, sharing a tiny space with family, friends, or strangers and adding to a sense of disarray and instability.

Students experiencing housing insecurity tend to move around more and change schools more often. Within one school year, 41 percent of students experiencing homelessness will attend two schools; 28 percent will attend three or more.[20] Adjusting to a new school culture, acclimating to new teacher expectations, and creating new friendships, all while attempting to catch up on previously taught material, can be extremely difficult. These students might be sharing a bed with parents and siblings, not getting enough nutritious food to eat, or living in a shelter. Enduring these types of high-level stress makes it difficult for kids to learn and concentrate in today's typical academic setting.

Trauma at Home

The outlook for students experiencing other forms of trauma is similarly bleak. Forty-six million young people are survivors of trauma.[21] This means that approximately one out of every four children attending school has been exposed to a traumatic event. Just think about this fact for a second: a quarter of students in any school or classroom has experienced trauma. Some of these students may be in the middle of experiencing an ongoing trauma, yet they're still getting to school, trying to interact with students and teachers and make it through the day. In addition, teenagers are three times more likely than younger children to suffer multiple victimizations by multiple perpetrators. Whether the distressing experience stems from a sick family member, homelessness, poverty, immigration status, violence, or sexual assault, the effects are deep and wide reaching. Research has demonstrated that trauma affects brain structure and function, learning, cognitive development, social and emotional development, behavior, and physical health. All of these are critical factors in both academic achievement and life success, factors we need to keep in mind as we develop new school structures and implement new teaching methodologies.

Unfortunately, these types of issues—uncertainty, violence, and fear—aren't limited to a student's home. We'd all like to think of school as a refuge, a place where students can learn, socialize, experiment, and grow—all without judgment or condemnation. But today, the reality is often very different.

Stresses at School

Students are now tested more often than ever before and are expected to participate in team sports, extracurriculars, and internships, all while being reminded that if they don't or can't perform, their future could slip away. For many young people, measurable success is emphasized at every level, causing students to fixate on the kind of external validation that comes with a perfect grade. For those students, college acceptance has become a life-long inflection point, a make-or-break moment, that determines the next fifty, sixty, or seventy years of their life. A lousy grade or failed experiment has become a fatal blow to future hopes and dreams. All too often, this type of pressure is being put on children and young adults—ten-, twelve-, or fifteen-year-olds who are still developing their personalities, social skills, and cognitive functioning. Understandably, this emphasis on test scores and GPA has a serious cost.

Education's obsession with testing is contributing to the rise of anxiety and depression in many young people. Jean Twenge, psychologist and author of *iGen*, says that by focusing on test scores and other extrinsic goals, we're encouraging children to measure their value by material gains and public opinion. But it's difficult to convince students of the value of old-school ideals like integrity or citizenship, as well as the benefits of finding an appropriate life philosophy, when they're more worried about getting into the right college and making piles of money. Studying trends observed over a fifty-year period, the Higher Education Research Institute found that college freshman are more concerned about "being well-off financially" than they are about building character.[22] This relates directly to my earlier point about students lacking independence, perseverance, and social skills.

Although the pressures of testing and academic perfection have serious costs—just think of the opening story of Cameron Lee, the Palo Alto student who took his own life—the truth is, other factors are also adding to the stress and anxiety children feel in our schools. In many schools, these factors include shifting classroom demographics that alter the ways we need to teach, and troubling national trends that too often have made school a physically dangerous place.

Changing Classroom Demographics

Increasingly, families are moving away from the suburbs and rural areas in favor of cities, where there are more jobs, but less access to nature and safe spaces to play. In addition, our classrooms have become ever more diverse, racially, culturally, and linguistically. The National Center for Education Statistics reports that by the year 2025, Latinx youth will account for close to 30 percent of all students. Conversely, the proportion of White students is expected to drop to 46 percent. African American enrollment will remain at 15 percent for the next several decades; Asian/Pacific Islander students will make up 6 percent and Native American students 1 percent; and the proportion of mixed-race students will increase to 4.5 percent. In eighty-three of our nation's largest cities, students of color make up a majority of the student body.[23] Diversity isn't bad, of course. It helps broaden students' experiences, increases acceptance and understanding, and makes all of us better collaborators.

Diversity is absolutely a positive, one we should value and encourage. But it does bring new challenges in our classrooms—and we need to provide our teachers with strategies and skills to address them.

It's also important to note that these more diverse schools tend to have higher populations of low-income students. And although cities may experience the greatest shifts, these demographic changes are taking place in communities across the country, even in smaller towns that were once racially homogenous.[24] In education, this transition is especially difficult for teachers who are used to teaching in a way that recognizes and understands a homogenous population. As a population shifts, teachers need to learn and incorporate new ways of relating to and teaching students, different ways of communicating and connecting. And let's be honest, change is difficult. Change is stressful. We often transmit this stress to students, whether we intend to or not. Change may also cause friction among groups in a school, helping create a more stressful environment. So, although growing diversity is a very real positive, it's also adding to the uncertainty and anxiety many of our students are feeling at school.

No Longer a Safe Space

With active shooter drills and an increase in security guards, checkpoints, and armed teachers, there are ample reasons for our students to feel anxious at school. This, in turn, affects their ability to learn and thrive in an educational environment. As we attempt to address these growing safety concerns, we must also keep in mind how these threats affect students' mental and physical health.

EXPERT IM

If a child doesn't feel safe at school, nothing productive will happen in that child's life that day.

—Dr. Brad Breedlove
Chief academic officer, Union County Public Schools, North Carolina

Since Columbine, gun violence on school grounds has become an unfortunate reality. There have been at least 111 school shootings in America since 1970. Over this fifty-year span, 202 people were killed and 454 were injured.[25] The violence has spiked in recent years, with tragic incidents such as the shootings at Marjorie Stoneman Douglas, Sandy Hook, and Santa Fe High School. These events have rocked our communities and inspired students to start the March for Our Lives movement to challenge gun laws. Yet active shooter scenarios aren't the only types of violence that occur in and around schools. There are targeted attacks, gang violence, and suicides to contend with as well. Or a student might simply bring a weapon to school to show off to his or her friends. And what about sporting events? Sadly, the threat of violence exists even outside normal school hours. Since 2013, gunfire has broken out at school sporting events at least 108 times.[26] On top of all this, we have to worry about violence inciting more violence, as young assailants often draw influence from prior school shootings. These are truly frightening numbers. Whether we're talking about gunfire, rioting, or bullying, all educators need to realize that as Union County Public Schools administrators told me, "School safety is our number-one priority."

An Ongoing Crisis

We as education professionals need to address the conditions that are creating this crisis and help kids develop the skills to navigate and contend with coming realities. From both a personal and professional perspective, nearly all of us have struggled with how to help children manage stress and anxiety in their lives. And to be fair, the increase in rates of mental and behavioral health diagnoses may be influenced by the fact that it has become more socially acceptable to talk about them. We are beginning to appropriately address mental health as both a developmental and medical problem that lies along a continuum.

I've experienced this in my own family. One of my sons struggles with extreme anxiety. It affects his ability to stay focused at work and in his personal relationships. His children are now exhibiting similar characteristics. In fact, five of my thirteen grandchildren have some form of behavioral health issue. On the milder end of that continuum is my granddaughter who has attention-deficit disorder (ADD). In the middle are two of my grandchildren who have serious anxiety disorders. At the severe end of the continuum are my two grandchildren who were born to cocaine-addicted mothers and suffered from abuse in multiple foster homes before being adopted by my son. These boys have debilitating behavioral health issues that require intense psychotherapy.

Many of us face issues like these every day, both personally and professionally. And just as there are developmental and preventive practices for maintaining a healthy physiological lifestyle—related to diet, exercise, sleep, avoiding stressful situations, and so on—there are also developmental and preventive practices that promote mental and behavioral health.

In our schools, we've had to prioritize these practices and integrate them into our culture. This means that school boards and administrators have had to use increasingly scarce financial resources to hire social workers, counselors, psychologists, and other staff to support our teachers and building administrators. These expenditures have, in many districts, come at the cost of shifting to hiring fewer teachers and increasing class sizes. The impact of these shifts is obvious to any of us who have ever taught. In chapter 3, I'll explore better options for alleviating many of these problems, but for now this much should be obvious: the students we're educating today are not the same as those of even just ten years ago. So why are we still using many of the same school structures, classroom practices, and instructional methodologies from the last century? If students feel, experience, and learn differently, why are we doing the same things we've always done? These questions take on greater importance when we look at the world our children will inherit—a world that's becoming more automated and more data based, more competitive and more uncertain. This new world is the topic of the next chapter.

LESSONS FOR THE FUTURE

- Our students are suffering from one of the worst mental health epidemics to date. Nearly four million children have been diagnosed with anxiety, another two million are battling depression, and at least one in three children exhibits behavioral disorders.
- New technologies have made our students more anxious, fragile, and lonely. Because students rely so heavily on technology, they have fewer meaningful relationships, expect instant gratification, and are exposed to explicit content and harassment online. They also lack such skills as mediating their digital footprint, being a respectful digital citizen, and being able to constructively incorporate feedback.
- Changes in our students' home lives have affected their mental and behavioral coping skills. Children of overprotective parents are terrified of failure and rely on adults to solve their problems. Other domestic factors such as missing parents, homelessness, and trauma have lasting effects that affect learning and follow students throughout their lives.
- School is an increasingly stressful environment. By focusing on objectives such as test scores, we've reinforced the idea that a student's worth depends on external validation. On a positive note, discussing mental health has become more acceptable, which partly explains why we're seeing more diagnoses at school.
- Our students don't always feel safe at school. Their new reality includes school shootings, suicides, and other types of violence that occur on school property, where students either witness or hear about it. If student don't feel safe, they won't engage or excel in the classroom.

2

Their Future World

Imagine Googling the population of Amsterdam, New York, or the date of the first NBA basketball game without touching a keyboard or speaking a word. Imagine answering an email or ordering a pizza just by thinking it. You could be an expert in any subject and have the entire internet in your head. Sounds like science fiction.

But it's already possible.

When you talk to yourself, your brain transmits electrical signals to your vocal chords. Arnav Kapur, a graduate student at the MIT Media Lab, has now created a headset that reads these signals, sends them to a computer, and responds through vibrations transmitted to the inner ear.[1] Profiled on *60 Minutes*, Kapur answered such questions as "What is 45,689 divided by 67?" and "What is the largest city in Bulgaria?" just by thinking the questions (681.925 and Sofia, with a population of 1.1 million). Kapur truly amazed the *60 Minutes* crew, though, when he ordered a stack of pizzas to be delivered without saying a word or lifting a finger—he just thought it.

Good-bye iPhone. Hello wearable, mind-reading computers.

There have been many other recent advancements in artificial intelligence (AI), automation, and robotics. We now have a Google program that can diagnose more than fifty eye diseases with an error rate better than clinical experts. Similarly, AI and new imaging techniques can diagnose tumors as accurately as pathologists can, and much faster. A Chinese insurance company has been using algorithms to read facial expressions and determine whether loan applicants are being honest. And not only are computers currently better than humans at our most complex games—for example, Go, chess, and no-limit Texas hold 'em—but Google's DeepMind can now beat us at multiplayer video games. This means that it knows how to strategize and coordinate with other players as part of a team. If this isn't enough, computers can also write symphonies. In a recent study, listeners at the University of Oregon couldn't tell the difference between a Bach composition and a composition written by a computer program.[2]

Yes, machines are getting smarter and more capable. Last century, few people, besides assembly line workers, worried when robots started to appear in factories. But when robots and AI began to take white-collar jobs, more people noticed. There are two schools of thought on what effect this technology will have on the availability of jobs. One view, which I'll describe in the following paragraphs, is that technology will decimate the job market and lead to widespread unemployment.

Consider what Lawrence Summers, former treasury secretary and chief economist of the World Bank, wrote: "I expect that more than *one-third* of all men between 25 and 54 will be out of work at mid-century. Very likely more than half of men will experience a year of non-work at least one year out of every five."[3] Add to this the devastating impact the COVID-19 pandemic has had on employment. A study by economists at the University of Chicago estimated that 42 percent of pandemic-based layoffs—which have exceeded thirty-eight million people—will result in permanent job loss.[4] This means that because of accelerated automation and changed habits, sixteen million jobs may vanish in the span of two months, never to return. "I think we're in for a very long haul," commented Nicholas Bloom, one of the authors of the study. Indeed.

This is a grim perspective on our changing job market. And to be fair, there is some truth to it. In the years ahead, millions of professionals who thought their careers were protected from automation will discover that their jobs can be done by a machine, a bot, or an algorithm. Even now, it's hard to identify a career that isn't at risk of being supplanted by AI. Journalist? We're already seeing computers write headlines and provide sports news. How about architect? BIM (building information modeling) and VDC (virtual design and construction) programs are already designing buildings. Lawyer? There are multiple websites that use automation to help people write a will, file for divorce, or register a trademark. And what about medicine, one of the most respected and desirable occupations in the

US and the world? Supercomputers such as IBM's Watson are already reading radiology scans, invading the operating room, and assigning oncology therapies—in most cases, doing a significantly better job than their human counterparts. Basically, if an algorithm can be written to do the job, that job is gone.

But hold on just one moment. There is an equally valid counterpoint to this argument: lost jobs rarely equate to no jobs. Having studied the labor market for many years, I believe we have a bright future. It's a different future that will require different skills—skills that machines, software, and other forms of technology aren't able to emulate. The beneficiaries of these new jobs will be those who are able to use technology to augment their own skills in a way that elevates productivity, performance, and creativity. This transition is no different than the earlier transitions from an agrarian society to an industrial society and from an industrial society to a knowledge-based society.

Although many people expect rampant unemployment and extensive dislocation over the next couple of decades, these needn't come to pass if we understand both what the future looks like and what we need to do to prepare students for it. We must be aware of technological developments, changing demographics, and evolving job requirements. Once we acknowledge these trends, we can begin to frame what this wave of change means for students and for education.

Today's—and Tomorrow's—Career Landscape

Last century, when many workers landed their first "real" jobs, they often stayed with that same employer until they retired. Not so today. Many of the industries and larger companies that dominated the twentieth-century economy have been kneecapped by technology. In some cases, industries have been all but wiped out. In other cases, jobs have been shipped overseas. And in still other cases, computers and robots have replaced a large percentage of employees.

With budgets under intense pressure from rapidly changing economic forces, payroll has been reduced, and several traditional company benefits, such pensions and retiree health care, have shrunk or flat-out disappeared. What's more, many companies today avoid hiring people full-time to get around having to pay benefits. Can't afford to provide health care benefits? Cut employee hours or label employees as "independent contractors."[5]

Yet scores of new companies have cropped up that see automation and AI as opportunities, not misfortunes. These younger, entrepreneurial organizations lure employees with innovative, more cost-effective benefits—a flexible workweek, opportunities to telecommute, or on-site wellness programs, to name just a few. Employees trade company loyalty for the opportunity to work in a fast-paced environment where leadership is distributed, innovation and agency are expected, and interdisciplinary collaboration is the norm.

These companies purposefully remain nimble, as they regularly iterate and pivot to adapt to the changing technologies and economic forces around them. In this environment, career paths are murky at best, and far more employees cycle in and out as business models evolve and companies' needs change. This sounds like Start-Up 101—move fast, stay lean, disrupt. But now this agile model has been adopted by many large corporations that operate in traditional economic sectors.

Vanishing Jobs

Amazon has many businesses. It's a tech company, a cloud services provider, and an entertainment company. It's also the largest retailer in the world.[6] Amazon has more products than any other company to sell, but instead of you coming to the store to get those products, the people at Amazon have to deliver them to you—quickly. Truckloads of goods come in, and truckloads of goods go out. Just consider how complicated Amazon's warehouses must be. Products get stored, pulled, packaged, and labeled. And throughout this whole process, the company has virtually no warehouse workers. Everything is done by robots. The only human workers in the warehouses are the few people who run and repair the robots.

Currently, every major supermarket in the country is introducing similar technology.[7] A robot built by Boston Nova Robotics can scan the aisles of a supermarket, aiding retailers in logging grocery inventory. The robots are designed to move autonomously through a store, taking high-resolution pictures of the shelves. They then use a very complex AI engine that extracts data from those shelves, including product data, label data, and product organization. All this information is processed and analyzed instantaneously and supplied to store management.

Walmart, the largest employer in the United States with 1.5 million employees, is trying out these robots in seventy-five stores.[8] The overarching plan is that within the next three years, robots will be working in all of their stores. This means that Walmart may lay off a significant percentage of their workforce in that time period.

This shift isn't taking place only in retail. Driverless cars, trucks, and airplanes will eventually eliminate jobs for contract drivers, taxi drivers, truckers, and pilots. This represents millions of jobs across the US, some with high salaries. The same thing is happening in construction, with robot "masons" able to lay bricks and blocks ten times faster than a team of human masons. And in agriculture, one of our oldest and most entrenched business sectors, robots can now analyze the size and health of plants and can harvest crops such as tomatoes, strawberries, and grapes. The following is a small sample of industries that will be affected by the adoption of AI-driven automation:

- Agriculture
- Construction trades
- Finance
- Food service
- Law enforcement
- Manufacturing
- Medicine
- Retail
- Transportation and delivery

In all of these industries, computers and robots offer overwhelming advantages. They don't need to be paid. They don't need health insurance. They don't get sick or take vacations. And they perform consistently at high levels of efficiency and precision. It's inevitable that as automation technologies become more mainstream and affordable, companies will choose them for cost savings and quality assurance. As alarming as these changes may seem, they are an early indicator of how machines and humans will need to learn to coexist in tomorrow's workplace. And make no mistake, this will be a beneficial union, offering new opportunities to those who have the ability to use technology to augment their own capabilities.

The Augmentation Age

I don't need to tell you how radically technology has changed the way we work and live. Most of us remember what it was like for us or our parents to book travel through a travel agent. Or to deposit checks inside a bank, handing deposit forms to a human teller. Or to page through the phone book to find businesses and call them on our corded phones. "Many people have heard of Moore's Law," says Jeff Brown, technology executive and editor for Rogue Economics. "Every 18 months computer processing power doubles. And each time, we get extraordinary improvements in technology."[9] This has been going on since the late 1960s. Brown continues, "In the early stages of exponential growth—say, the first 20 doublings—the change isn't dramatic at all. But when you get to the twenty-sixth doubling, you reach the 'elbow' of the curve. And after that, the progress shoots straight up."

Although it may seem surprising, right now, we're at the elbow.

As most of us are aware, AI—computer systems able to perform tasks such as visual perception, writing algorithms, speech recognition, decision-making, and translation between languages—is the driving force behind automation today. AI already exists in our personal lives. Apple's Siri and Amazon's Alexa have become indispensable virtual assistants for many people. Every day, it seems, we're creeping closer to the holy grail of AI: creating software that comes close to mimicking human intelligence. Google, Facebook, Amazon, Apple, Microsoft, and other companies are spending billions trying to develop machines that will possess human-like intelligence and common sense. With the Industrial Revolution, machines brought productivity gains and physical support to manual laborers. In the information age, they replaced human laborers. In its earliest forms, AI brought efficiencies to knowledge workers, who have historically been higher paid. Now, in the augmentation age, AI is threatening to replace the knowledge workers—everyone from computer programmers to doctors to financial analysts.

But this is not just a simple case of technology replacing us. Humans will still be necessary in many capacities. It's far more likely, at least in the next couple of decades, that automation and AI will augment our capabilities. We already experience this type of augmentation with our smartphones, which by giving us billions of facts and resources at our fingertips help free up brain space. We don't need to remember birthdays, phone numbers, or who starred in *The Lord of the Rings*; we can just look up these details anywhere, at any time.

EXPERT IM

There are some skills that are uniquely human. Machines won't take over interactions or human engagement. Therefore, we need to make sure our schools are creating learning opportunities that support the development of interaction, collaboration, and the building of beautiful things.

—Karen Cator
President and CEO, Digital Promise

This is what computer scientists call "passive" augmentation, the first stage of cognitive augmentation. The next two stages are the "generative" and the "intuitive."[10] As I mentioned, machines and AI are in the passive stage now. The passive stage, as we see with Google and Siri, is characterized by what is referred to as *recognition intelligence.* These are algorithms that recognize patterns. The generative stage will come when machines can make inferences or deductions from data. In the generative stage, computers will take human instructions or suggestions and then design a solution, taking into account human goals and constraints. For example, consider an engineering firm tasked with designing a bridge. Today, a team still needs months, even with technological support, to work through computations, codes, and specifications based on parameters they input, such as span length, material, load capacity, traffic volume, and climate. It has been estimated that by 2030, an engineer will complete the entire design—and offer equally well considered options—in a matter of minutes.

The intuitive stage will arrive, further in the future, when machines can reason with far greater subtlety than they can now. Machines will start making decisions for us, beginning a push toward those Skynet-like systems that have been vilified in apocalyptic science fiction.

More optimistically, human augmentation will occur as a function of people and robots partnering and collaborating to think, work, and learn. No doubt, the skills of the future will be vastly different from those of today. But if humans continue to do what they're good at (awareness, perception, and decision-making) and robots do what they're good at (performing repetitive tasks with precision), we can continue to coexist and even thrive.

Many of these changes have been extensively reported. People have been ringing the AI bell for years both in books such as *Race against the Machine* by Erik Brynjolfsson and Andrew McAfee and *Superintelligence* by Nick Bostrom, and in articles in the *New York Times*, the *Atlantic*, the *Economist*, and other outlets. What's less well publicized are the many demographic changes—some as radical as the technological changes—that are coming over the next decade.

Changing Demographics

In the United States—and in many other developed countries—we're facing three major demographic trends that will alter our world and affect students in the future: a shrinking middle class, an aging population and shrinking workforce, and an inability of young adults to meet traditional "adult" milestones, which creates a high degree of social inertia or stagnation. Let's start with the coming changes in class distribution.

The Shrinking Middle Class

Until about 1970, the median income for all workers showed a healthy, consistent increase. Thanks to new technologies and new overseas markets, the rising tide lifted almost every boat from about 1950 to 1970. Then something happened. Starting in the late twentieth century, a large segment of the workforce was excluded from this economic expansion because of such factors as automation, outsourcing, and global competition.[11] Figure 2.1 shows how this trend has continued since 2000 and is projected to worsen by 2030.

As the years progress, there are more entry-level jobs. How can this be if automation is taking away so many low-paying jobs? The same tech-driven economy creates more jobs at the top. And that group at the top needs people to clean their houses. They need nannies and other help with child care. They need someone to mow their lawn, deliver their groceries, and cook their food. This group at the top has created an enormous service sector. The catch, of course, is that service sector jobs don't pay enough for a person or family to be financially independent. Regrettably, this means that we're moving toward a much more polarized nation of haves and have-nots. This shift, in turn, creates a serious problem for education. Public education has always been designed to prepare students for the middle class, but

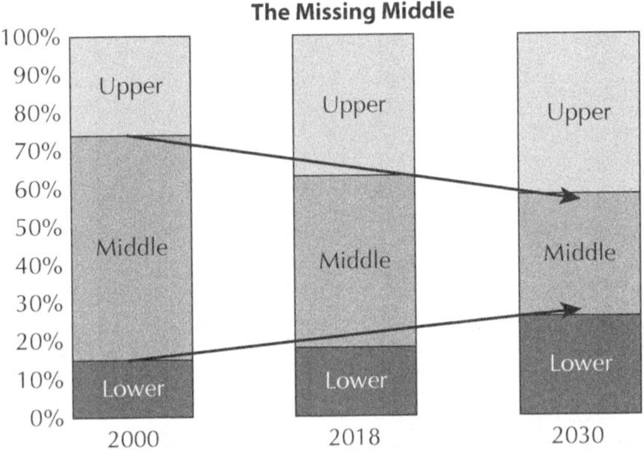

FIGURE 2.1 Class Trends in the United States: The Missing Middle

now our middle class is disappearing. And to compound problems, as our middle class is disappearing, our population is also aging.

An Aging Population Equals a Contracting Workforce

Support ratio is an economic term that refers to ways the government supports its citizens. There are two kinds of support: direct government benefits and indirect government benefits. We all receive indirect government benefits. We drive on roads and highways that governments have built, we enjoy tax-funded parks and meeting places, and derive safety from our federally supported military.

Direct government benefits refer to what the government is doing for you personally—either giving you money or paying for something for you. Among all Americans under the age of eighteen—74.2 million people—23 percent receive more direct government benefits than they pay in.[12] For this, I'm grateful. These are all "our" children, and they need our help to survive and prosper. How do they receive direct government benefits? For most kids in this age group, it's through schooling, which is funded by local, state, and federal tax dollars. This is a wonderful benefit that has helped the United States become the most innovative, most economically advantaged country in the world. But 74.2 million is a lot of people.

Another group of people who typically receive more direct government support than they pay in are those age sixty-five and older. At this age, most

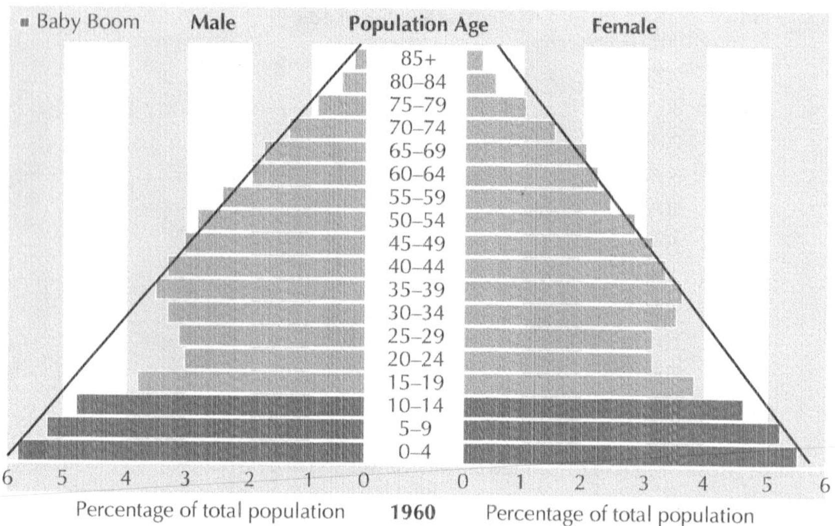

FIGURE 2.2 The Support Ratio in 1960

Source: Daggett, W. (2016). *Making schools work: A vision for college and career ready learning* (pp 21–22). Rexford, NY: International Center for Leadership in Education.

Americans have left the workforce and are collecting Social Security, Medicare, and Medicaid. I'm certainly not saying that they don't deserve these benefits—they paid into the programs throughout their working lives. But this is another forty-five million people. Between these two groups, that's nearly 120 million people who are receiving direct benefits.

And this is the issue.

When these programs were created, there were significantly more young people than old, and especially working-age people. Thus, the thinking was, there were plenty of folks who could contribute productively to society, pay taxes, and fund social programs for the retired and underprivileged. Figure 2.2 shows our population dynamics in 1960.

The distribution looks like a pyramid, with a large number of working-age people helping support social programs. As shown in Figure 2.3, our pyramid has now morphed into a rectangle, with the aging baby boomers retiring from the workforce and tapping Social Security, Medicare, and Medicaid.

It's estimated that by 2030, the number of people sixty-five and older will jump to eighty million. They'll live longer, on average until eighty. And

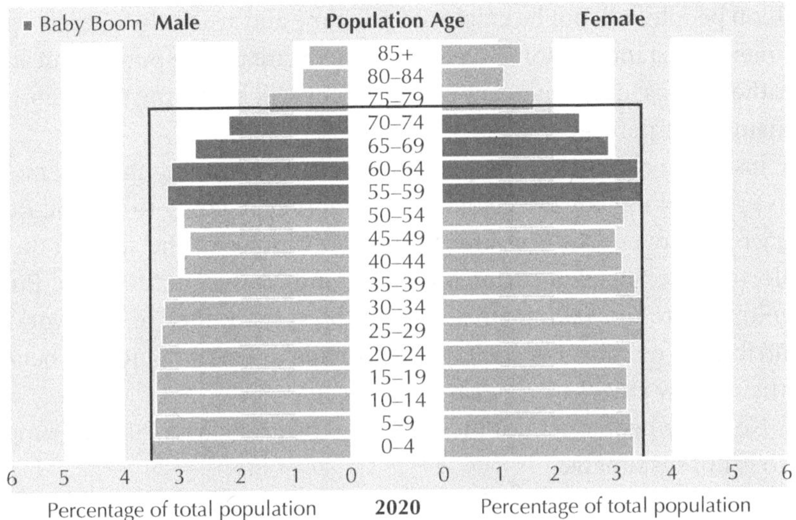

FIGURE 2.3 The Support Ratio in 2020

Source: Daggett (2016).

because they'll be an incredible lobbying force, they're likely to push the government to maintain—or increase—their benefits.

Exacerbating this economic squeeze, 127 million working-age Americans—or 39.7 percent of those in this eighteen-to-sixty-five age group—are not working. They're not paying tax on income, and some are receiving government support through Medicaid, Social Security disability programs, or college financial assistance. That's 127 million people! In other words, 246 million Americans in total, or 76.8 percent, are not working full-time, and some are receiving, or have at one time received, government support.

There's one final group that I must add to the mix, and it includes many of you reading this book: public employees. Public employees, and certainly educators, are invaluable workers and essential contributors to this nation, its economy, and its overall well-being. Yet we must keep in mind that taxpayers are covering 100 percent of our salaries, as well as the salaries of all public workers. Mathematically speaking, public sector employees receive more in direct government paid salaries and benefits than they pay into the system through taxes. That's 22.4 million of us, or 7 percent of the total US population.

What all of this analysis means, should our present economic trends persist into the future, is that 91 percent of the US population, or 303.6

million people, will not be employed full-time and are likely to receive government assistance of some type, from Medicare to free public education. In other words, only 9 percent of Americans will be paying to support the remaining 91 percent.

Just to be clear: These 91 percent are NOT scamming the system. The kids aren't taking advantage of the system; they're going to school. Retiring workers over sixty-five aren't taking advantage of the system; they're collecting the Social Security, Medicare, and Medicaid due them. Public employees are not taking advantage of the system; they're hardworking, contributing members of society who provide a wealth of indirect benefits to their fellow citizens.

No, these people are not the problem. The problem is that this support ratio is not sustainable.

Growing Social Inertia

In an extensive study, UBS found that millennials are significantly more risk-averse than previous generations.[13] According to statistics, they're taking longer to get married and to establish a career. Similarly, according to Pew Research Center analysis, younger generations are less likely to have the three things most commonly associated with adulthood—a spouse, a home, or a child.[14]

But even without these traditional "anchors," twenty-somethings are moving less than past generations. In 2016, only 20 percent of millennial-age adults reported having lived at a different address one year earlier. The one-year migration rates were higher for previous generations, usually hovering closer to 30 percent.

In addition, as I mentioned in the introduction, today's young adults are also more likely to return to their parents' home for an extended period of time. According to a Pew Research Center analysis of census data, 15 percent of twenty-five-to-thirty-five-year-old adults were living in their parents' home. This is a 50 percent increase over the number of Gen Xers who lived at home at the same age, and nearly double the share of the Silent Generation who lived at home at a comparable age.[15]

Some might say this is a millennial problem. But the reality is, this trend is unlikely to subside, especially with the growing pressures of student debt, high housing costs, and a decreasing number of good entry-level jobs. And once the pandemic struck in 2020, young adults began migrating home in unprecedented numbers. They fled the cities for the suburban or rural homes they grew up in, some bringing partners or pets along with them. As many parents and educators are learning, the idea of living at home through one's twenties has now become so normalized that it has spawned its own generational title, the "boomerang generation," and its own syndrome, "failure to launch."

Success Skills for the Future

In the future, more careers will be created in entrepreneurial companies than in large corporations. As we know, these jobs require certain attitudes, mindsets, and behaviors to navigate both less structured environments and less obvious career paths.

In specific terms, according to a Bureau of Labor Statistics report on the fastest-growing occupations, 81 percent of job growth will be in service-providing sectors. Health care and social assistance jobs will account for over a third of the jobs added.[16] Success in these roles will often rely heavily on strong interpersonal and noncognitive skills. And on the more technical side of health care jobs, success will also require data analytics skills. Outside the health care and social assistance categories, jobs that will also see significant growth include statisticians, operations research analysts, personal financial advisors, cartographers and photogrammetrists, interpreters and translators, forensic science technicians, and web developers. All of these jobs require agility and fluency with data and robust analytical skills. Those who occupy these roles will also need to know how to take or advise action with the data they collect, monitor, investigate, or evaluate.

To assist in defining the skills that help fulfill these jobs, the McKinsey group conducted a study on the changes in work requirements between now and 2030.[17] To collect data, they surveyed a hundred small companies, a hundred medium-size companies, and a hundred large companies. Figure 2.4 presents the results of the study.

What McKinsey discovered is that there will be a 15 percent decline in the need for basic cognitive skills. The reason for this decline is that you can Google all the facts and rules you need to know. McKinsey also found that there would be a 14 percent decline in manual and physical skills. These two skill categories are where we spent almost all of our time and resources in

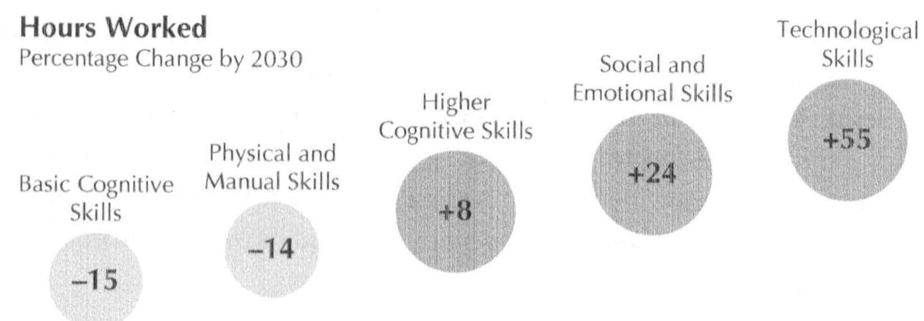

FIGURE 2.4 Skills for the Future

Source: Adapted from Bughin et al., "Skill Shift: Automation and the Future of the Workforce," McKinsey Global Institute, May 23, 2018. Retrieved from https://www.mckinsey.com/featured-insights/future-of-work/skill-shift-automation-and-the-future-of-the-workforce.

our schools during the last decade. Now, I want to be clear, no one is saying that basic cognitive skills are not important. They are. The fact is, you can't get to the right side of this figure if you don't have basic cognitive skills. The mistake has been telling learners that all they need to do is get through the next test and make it to the next grade. That's just not true anymore.

So, according to McKinsey, what skills will students need to succeed in the future? Higher cognitive skills, social and emotional learning, and technological skills. Social and emotional skills—or social and emotional learning (SEL), as it's commonly called—is more important than ever before. Don't worry if you're not an expert on SEL. We'll cover it in depth in the next chapter. And to clarify, technological skills don't refer to the ability to use Microsoft Excel or operate a computer. Instead, these entail a deeper understanding of how to harness technology in order to innovate, solve problems, find resources, or augment other skills. Think of big data and data analytics. Data analytics isn't math or language arts or science. It's a combination of disciplines that enables us to translate data into actionable information. So data analytics—and technological skills in a broader sense—is about learning how to ask questions, investigate, use models, and determine a path forward.

EXPERT IM

We want kids graduating with the skill set to be able to work as a team and to have the kind of the soft nonacademic skills that jobs and businesses will still need in a hundred years. But I also don't want to lose sight of the fact that we want graduates to be great people who are improving communities.

—Dr. Andrew G. Houlihan
Superintendent of Union County School District, North Carolina

My guess is that for many of us these proficiencies still sound too general. Let's break these categories down into more granular, specific skills. As various experts, studies, and the team at ICLE see it, the following are the specific skills that we need to address in our classrooms today:

- Students will need to **analyze vast amounts of data** quickly and efficiently. For them to be able to do this, schools must start teaching data analytics, which is simply evaluating data using analytical and logical reasoning to form a conclusion.
- Students increasingly will need to **communicate through charts, tables, and graphs**. We've got to teach kids how to understand and build tables, graphs, and charts, especially in the workplace. This is particularly important in translating data into easily understood information, concepts, or stories.
- Students will need to **know basic statistics**. Today, statistics is typically not taught until college. But looking at employment trends, we know this won't cut it anymore. Figure out how you can integrate statistics into your math curriculum in K–12 and then make it a new core subject in high school mathematics. Consider where else statistics pop up—sociology, biology, and history, to name just some subjects—and take an interdisciplinary approach to its incorporation for added real-world relevance and interest for students.
- Because we live in such a technologically rich environment, **technical reading and technical writing** skills will be critical for all students. Don't make the mistake of confusing technical reading with basic literacy. Understanding technical manuals requires a different form of comprehension than appreciating literature.
- Voice recognition software also will improve dramatically in the immediate future. Virtual assistants Siri, Cortana, and the others will become

very, very precise. This means that students must **learn how to speak clearly and in technical terms**—in other words, employ technical speaking. And that skill is not taught at all. You might get it indirectly if you take many engineering courses, but it's not being taught to everybody. This is now also true with mind-reading computers like the device highlighted in the chapter introduction. When these types of devices are widespread, how precisely students think will be as important as how precisely they talk.

- To win well-paying jobs of the future, workers must be more effective and adept than machines. They will need to **competently and flexibly use a variety of technical knowledge**.
- Because machines are better than humans at defined tasks and calculations, students must develop **independent thinking and problem-solving skills**—the types of skills that will help them solve novel problems. These skills include understanding where to find information, synthesizing information, the ability to prototype, and seeing failure as an incremental learning experience that leads to success.
- Because of the overwhelming amount of information that's now available, the **ability to manage one's cognitive load** has become vital to success. What information is true? What's false or misleading? Which information is the "signal" and which is the "noise"? What needs to be remembered, and what can be left to phones, tablets, computers, and other augmentation devices? What email or other electronic messages are critical? These are questions that students will need to answer to excel in the future workforce.
- Because people still need to work with other people, noncognitive skills based on **social and emotional learning** will bring tremendous value to employers. Collaborative skills—managing emotions, people management (leadership), trust building, showing empathy, and cultural awareness—will help employees work both on situated teams (teams whose members are all in one place) and on remote teams. As remote teams become more prevalent and team members need to make deep connections across time zones, these skills will become even more valued.
- There's no question that AI, algorithms, and automation are eating up jobs that rely on rules-based skills. Where these technologies are weak, however, is in such areas as **creative thinking, understanding**

ambiguity, and judging human desires. We'll still need deeply creative people to design the types of buildings, products, or experiences that bring joy. We'll still need a humanistic understanding to provide effective treatments or to react to unexpected events. In these ways, humans offer enhancements that technology will desperately need.

In short, success and self-sufficiency will increasingly depend on creating, evaluating, and analyzing material and applying solutions to real-world, unpredictable situations—often as part of a collaborative team. Today's children will be 2030s youngest workers and will succeed by being skilled in areas where technology on its own can't succeed, such as judging data for quality and interpreting outputs from an algorithm. This requires future students to be, above all, resourceful. As veteran educator and administrator Samuel Houston, paraphrasing an accomplished teacher named Grant Wiggins, told me: "Students today have to know what to do when they're not sure what to do." In other words, students need to be able to figure out a course of action in the face of unique problems and challenges.

What does all this mean for education? It means that we need to change our overarching approach, starting with rethinking our primary goal in preparing our students for *their* future.

Career Ready versus College Ready

In the twentieth century, before internet technologies turned everything we knew upside down, there was little difference between preparing students for college and preparing them for careers. The skills required to get to and excel in college and those required to excel in careers were almost the same. In other words, the twentieth-century economy was built on specific knowledge and area expertise that was applied to predictable circumstances. Careers often remained confined to one focus, one silo, one department. Thus the college prep model of teaching—where knowledge is gathered through and applied to one discipline—sufficiently prepared students for careers back in the day.

But as should be clear, kids now need different skills to succeed in the twenty-first century. College prep is focused on preparing students for success in higher education. Preparing students for jobs is not the same as preparing them for careers. Career and tech education prepares students for jobs. Preparing students for a career is significantly different from preparing them for either college or a job.

The Career Readiness Partner Council, formed in 2012, is a group of leaders from national education and workforce organizations seeking to clarify what it means to be not just job ready but also career ready. Here's their perspective: a career-ready person effectively navigates pathways that connect education and employment to achieve a fulfilling, financially secure, and successful career.[18] A career is more than just a job. Career readiness has no defined endpoint. To be career ready in our ever-changing global economy requires adaptability and a commitment to lifelong learning, along with mastery of key knowledge, skills, and dispositions that vary from one career to another and change over time as a person progresses along a developmental continuum.

EXPERT IM

In our polling, we've found that the idea that students need higher education to succeed has been on the decline. Many people believe it's not worth the investment. That's why the teaching of entrepreneurial skills has become a significant part of our polling. A lot of future talent probably won't end up in college.

—Katie Lyon
Managing director, higher education, Gallup

To be blunt, I believe that for many of our students a bachelor's degree has become a false premise and a broken promise. College is no longer the guaranteed gateway to a good job that will equip a graduate for lifelong self-sustainability. Neither is the assumption, at least in terms of employment and being economically independent, that more college is better than less college. A Tennessee study showed that the average salary of the state's graduates of two-year colleges is higher than that of four-year college graduates.[19] Why? Soaring demand for workers in technology fields. Moreover, the cost of earning a four-year or advanced degree has risen, in many cases, beyond any reasonable assessment of return on investment. To see how much the cost of a four-year college degree has increased, see figure 2.5.

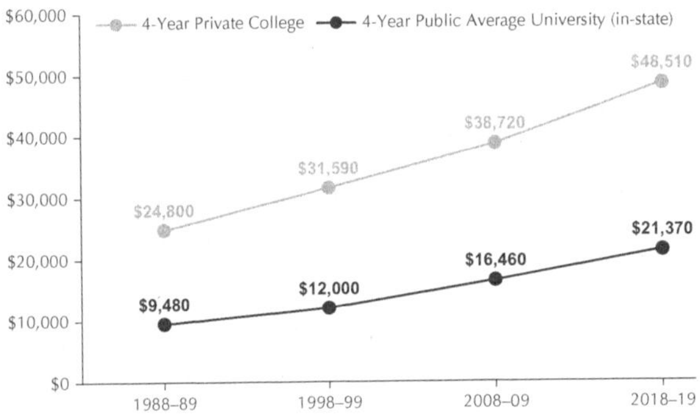

FIGURE 2.5 Figure 2.5 The Rising Cost of College: Average Published Tuition and Fees Plus Room and Board, in 2018 Dollars, 1988–90 to 2018–19

Source: Adapted from College Board, Trends in College Pricing. Retrieved from https://trends.collegeboard.org/sites/default/files/2018-trends-in-college-pricing.pdf

In *Most Likely to Succeed: Preparing Our Kids for the Innovation Era*, Tony Wagner, an expert-in-residence at Harvard University's Innovation Lab, explains that graduates are not only in debt but also underprepared for the workforce. "We hear from employers regularly about how ill-prepared graduates are, even graduates from elite colleges, to take on workplace responsibilities. How creativity and imagination have been schooled out of them. How they seem to be allergic to unstructured problems. How they seek constant micromanagement and the workplace equivalent of a daily, even hourly, grade."[20]

Yes, four-year college remains important and appropriate for many students. But not for all. Regardless of whether a student chooses to attend college, our ultimate goal as educators remains the same: we're aiming to get students into successful, self-sufficient lives, which usually come by way of a career. Today, college is more and more just one choice among many on the road to success. It's time we recognize that our twentieth-century instructional model simply won't cut it for twenty-first-century career preparation. We must figure out how to promote the academics that underpin "career ready" to be on equal footing with the academics that underpin "college ready."

It's our job as educators to cultivate critical thinking skills, encourage creativity, nurture life skills, and instill confidence in our students, supporting our students in becoming resourceful and independent. One could argue that these qualities are—college degree or not—the true path to success. Not every student can, will, or should go to college. Our young people, however, deserve the opportunities to learn and develop the abilities, mindsets, and confidence to reach their highest potential. This is the most certain path to making the students of today into successful, responsible, self-reliant adults and citizens who contribute to the betterment of society.

Future School Leadership

Labor and employment experts are predicting that 85 percent of the jobs today's students will be doing in 2030 have not yet been invented.[21] Because the world is evolving at such an accelerated pace, the skills needed will be ever changing, and an employee's ability to gain new skills will be valued more highly than how much knowledge he or she can retain. Today's students and tomorrow's workers will need to be adept at accessing information and skilled in improvising and adapting to new, immersive technologies.

Have our schools responded? Yes, they have. But are our efforts paying off? In most cases, we've added more tests, requirements, regulations, and rules while continuing to prepare students for a world that no longer exists. We've doubled down on the past rather than focusing on the future. We're no longer sending our students off to yesterday's large corporations where they would steadily climb the ranks for the duration of a career, with guaranteed benefits awaiting them at retirement. We cannot, in good conscience, continue to use yesterday's model to educate our children for tomorrow's challenges.

Today's principal or superintendent must be prepared to focus time, attention, and effort on changing what students are taught, how they're taught, and what they're learning. This formidable challenge demands a new breed of school leader, a person with skills and knowledge far greater than those expected of the "school manager" of the past. Which leads us to an essential question: *What do today's successful school leaders need to know and be able to do?*

To find the answer, read on.

LESSONS FOR THE FUTURE

- Jobs that require following complicated directions or clear rules are at risk of being taken over by technology, and especially AI. Up until now, someone could make a good living doing a "rules-based" job. Many of these jobs are now at risk. If an algorithm can be written to do the job, that job is gone. The good news? As jobs disappear, new jobs are created.
- In its earliest forms, AI brought efficiencies to knowledge workers, who have historically been higher paid. Now AI is threatening to replace many of these workers. But this is not a simple case of technology just replacing us. Humans will still be necessary in many capacities. It's far more likely, at least in the next couple of decades, that automation and AI will augment our capabilities.
- Three major demographic trends that will alter our world and affect students in the future include a shrinking middle class, an aging population and shrinking workforce, and an inability of young adults to meet traditional adult milestones.
- In the future, success and self-sufficiency will increasingly depend on creating, evaluating, and analyzing material and applying solutions to real-world, unpredictable situations—often as part of a collaborative team. This requires such skills as problem solving, critical thinking, collaboration, and social and emotional intelligence.
- Four-year college remains important and appropriate for many students, but not every student can, will, or should go to college. This means that as educators we must make students career ready. To be career ready in our ever-changing global economy requires adaptability and a commitment to lifelong learning.

3

Developing the Whole Child

A boy, Alex, shows up for the first day of kindergarten looking worried. The other kids are also nervous, but they quickly acclimate. Instead of getting past it, though, Alex hides all day under his desk, gripping the metal legs until his knuckles turn white.

Three middle school students, two boys and a girl, stay after school in their language arts classroom to continue an in-class discussion about their parents' divorces. It soon becomes an impromptu club; the busy teacher needs time to plan his lessons, but realizes that these kids have never had a place to open up and share.

A freshman in high school, Maria, had always received good grades. But suddenly she starts failing her classes and shutting out her family. It takes her parents several weeks to realize the full extent the problem: she has an eating disorder.

Alice, a second-grader, seems to be going out of her way to antagonize her peers—sitting on them during circle time, yelling insults at lunchtime. The school staff struggles to help her channel those negative interactions into the positive attention she really wants.

Do any of these situations sound familiar? Over the past couple of years, I've been asking educators in urban, suburban, and rural schools across the country whether they're experiencing an increase in behavioral mental health issues with students.

The response is loud, clear, and consistent: yes!

Teachers and support staff can give hundreds of similar examples of dealing with student behavioral health issues daily. In my conversations with teachers, counselors, and principals around the country, they tell me that these issues have been increasing in recent years. Yet, too often, the way teachers are being evaluated, or expected to "do their job," isn't changing. Districts' growing focus on evaluation requirements has only reinforced for teachers that they should pay more attention to academic performance than to anything else. They're constantly feeling the pressure to push their students to the next test and the next grade. Too often, evaluations fail to take into account that teachers have to meet these metrics *while* maintaining order in classrooms with children whose behavior is drastically different from that of students just five or ten years ago. I hear the following over and over again from teachers: student issues, from disruptive behavior to lack of focus to mental health concerns, have become a huge obstacle for them in "doing their job."

These concerns, of course, are not misplaced. Clearly, there are growing mental health—or what psychologists call "behavioral health"—issues with our kids. As we've learned in previous chapters, our kids and their world are changing dramatically because of technological advancements, cultural shifts, and global issues. In this new reality, our students have new needs that can be incredibly challenging to meet within the context of the school building or the classroom. Many of these needs *can* be met, and the possibility of future success bolstered, through what's commonly known as *social and emotional learning (SEL).* Our research and conversations at the International Center for Leadership in Education (ICLE) show that SEL is proving critical to students' success in school and beyond.

In this chapter, we'll dig into how best to address the behavioral health issues our students are facing. We'll look at the challenges in incorporating an SEL initiative, the key features of a successful initiative, and the initial steps in implementing this initiative throughout a district or school. In addition, I'll provide a detailed rubric that can guide you and your team through every step in creating a sustainable SEL initiative—one that works at every education level and in all types of schools. But first, let's define exactly what we at ICLE mean by SEL. We need a uniform and consistent understanding of the term; otherwise, SEL becomes all things to all people and loses its central focus.

From Instinctive Knowledge to Defined Skills

SEL is the process people use to understand their emotions, manage and control their feelings, make responsible decisions, identify and master goals, connect with others, develop empathy and understanding for others, and foster friendships and other positive relationships. That's a mouthful! In some ways, controlling feelings may seem basic, but putting language to the process can be complicated. SEL, though, can be broken down into age-appropriate steps and then taught to others, just like the process of reading or addition or playing a sport. These basic skills can and should be built over time. We don't expect kids to pick up a basketball and suddenly make a free throw, but we too often expect kids to show a mastery of their emotions the first time they sit in a classroom. These emotional and behavioral skills need to be taught and reinforced over and over again, just as do skills like dribbling or passing or shooting.

The ideas behind SEL are not new; they have always been part of our unwritten or hidden curriculum. But as the needs of students have skyrocketed, with an accompanying national call for SEL in our schools, identifying and defining the skills students must attain in order to deal effectively and ethically with daily tasks has become more critical.

For this reason, creating standards for a social and emotional development curriculum is just as important as for an academic curriculum. Every teacher in every grade in every school district knows the core competencies and standard skills they're expected to guide their students toward achieving. And although the phrase *social and emotional learning* is being increasingly used in schools, I respectfully suggest that we need a better shared definition of the term and understanding of the key concepts in order to effectively address SEL in our schools.

Organizations such as Collaborative for Academic, Social and Emotional Learning (CASEL) and a national commission created by the Aspen Institute have compiled a list of skills and competencies that constitute behavioral health, as Joseph A. Durlak, Celene E. Domitrovich, Roger P. Weissberg, and Thomas P. Gullotta explain in the *Handbook of Social and Emotional Learning: Research and Practice.*[1] The five core competencies for behavioral health are self-awareness, self-management, social awareness, relationship skills, and responsible decision-making. The following are definitions of each competency:

- **Self-awareness:** understanding one's emotions, personal goals, and values and recognizing that thoughts, feelings, and actions are interconnected

- **Self-management:** possessing the skills necessary to regulate emotions and behaviors in order to achieve one's goals, such as delaying gratification, managing stress, controlling impulses, and persevering through challenges
- **Social awareness:** having respect for, empathizing with, and feeling compassion for people who have different backgrounds or cultures; recognizing social norms for behavior
- **Relationship skills:** communicating clearly, listening actively, cooperating, resisting inappropriate social pressure, negotiating conflict constructively, and seeking help when needed
- **Responsible decision-making:** making responsible decisions that consider ethical standards, safety concerns, and realistic evaluations of the consequences of various actions, and that take the health and well-being of self and others into consideration

The definitions here support what many teachers already instinctively understand. These skills are cognitive (the ability to focus, pay attention, and set goals); social and interpersonal (the ability to read social skills and cooperate); and emotional (the ability to manage emotions and cope).

But make no mistake: teaching these competencies is *not* about social engineering. This is about the mental health and future success of our children, of our upcoming parents, leaders, and citizens. We must be able to effectively measure growth of these competencies, monitor them, and continuously build them into the culture and curriculum in our schools in multiple ways. Comprehensive and sustained professional learning experiences for all staff are key to helping schools support students like the young child under the desk, the kids coming to chat with the teacher, the middle schooler with the eating disorder, the out-of-control second-grader, and every other student.

SEL Benefits All Students

Whether we are aware of it or not, our children are in a constant state of SEL, where their perceptions and experiences either support or undermine their healthy social-emotional development and capacity to learn and interact with others in general. Defining the skills helps us as educators act with intention to foster learning relationships and integrate SEL into academic settings. Doing so will simultaneously enhance learning, develop healthy social-emotional skills, prevent mental health issues, and prepare students for an economic environment that values collaboration and problem solving.

SEL and Academic Learning

Even students who are not at risk for major behavioral or mental health issues can benefit from SEL in the classroom. Until recently, our understanding of the brain has been that it's broken into three distinct parts with three distinct functions thought to be layered upon each other:

- **Layer 1.** The lowest level is the primitive brain, which manages our survival instinct (e.g., helps us respond to threats).
- **Layer 2.** The second level is the social, affective brain, which was understood to generate emotions that steer the survival process (e.g., sees threat, feels fear, runs).
- **Layer 3.** The top layer is the prefrontal cortex, the part of the brain divided into left and right hemispheres, which does all our high-level, abstract thinking. In the old paradigm, the prefrontal cortex was thought to be mostly separate from the survival and affective mechanisms of the brain.

The latest neuroscience, however, is challenging this old view of the distinct layers of the brain. Now we know that they're more connected than we once thought. As the affective neuroscientist, human development psychologist, and former public school teacher Mary Helen Immordino-Yang writes, "It is literally neurobiologically impossible to build memories, engage complex thoughts, or make meaningful decisions without emotions."[2] In other words, we can't separate emotional learning from academic learning.

EXPERT IM

It's absolutely essential that kids have both executive functioning and social emotional learning in order to be successful in adult life. Period. Research is unequivocal about that. But when kids lack those

> capabilities, we punish them. We would never say to a child struggling in reading or math, "You know what, you're not getting it. Go to the principal's office."
>
> —Shauna McDonald
> Executive director, Playworks Minnesota

The prefrontal cortex—where we contemplate math and philosophy, invent solutions, feel compassion, plan our future, and so on—is both a function and a driver of the survival and affective mechanisms of the brain. All three are interdependent processes: how we think relies on our survival and affective mechanisms, and these mechanisms also reorganize themselves in service of how we think.[3]

This new brain research tells us that how we think can change how we feel and can change our survival mechanism—for better or worse. What does this mean for educators? It means that learning doesn't only happen in the thinking brain; it also happens in the feeling and surviving brain. To teach well is to consider and address all three parts of the brain and how they work together to either support or undermine learning. We can teach in ways that literally augment intellectual capacity in the moment, or squash it.

No wonder SEL is so important. The brain research is clear: SEL is not separate from academic learning.

It *is* academic learning.

The Benefits of SEL for Diversity

In addition to addressing the underlying behavioral and mental health concerns of today's students and forming a core part of their academic learning, SEL is particularly important for fostering empathy in classrooms. Returning to the SEL skill set, social awareness and relationship skills create the kind of classroom setting where students can be aware of their differences and can celebrate them equally without privileging one over another.

In Tyrone Howard's book *All Students Must Thrive*, Patrick Carmangian, an associate professor at the University of San Francisco School of Education, notes that SEL should not be combined with so-called color-blind approaches in schools; the point is not to take away the differences between students in a way that minimizes core parts of their humanity. As Carmangian states, "Color-blind approaches to SEL compound the harm done by intersecting systems of oppression by placing the burden of responsibility for change on the people who are harmed the most—students of color, gender nonconforming youth, and young people whose families bear the brunt of economic disparities in underdeveloped communities."[4] Too often, a key component of social awareness—having compassion for people from different backgrounds or cultures—can turn into stereotyping or making condescending assumptions. Instead, active listening and respect for individual students' intersectional identities and lived experiences can help address needs in the classroom. That approach is critical for true SEL to occur.

By meeting students where they are, giving them the emotional tools they need in their academic learning, and helping them understand and communicate well with others—even those whose backgrounds are different from their own—SEL benefits students and educators alike. But how do we take these concepts and implement them in our classrooms? And is it possible to train teachers in a large-scale way across entire districts to benefit all students? Let's look at some best practices for implementing SEL, as well as some approaches that schools around the country use to make SEL a regular part of their curriculum.

Understanding the Behavioral Health Continuum

Intentionality is the key to effective SEL. We need to shift our mindsets from "What is wrong with this child?" to "What happened to this child?" The first approach places blame on the child and assumes that he or she has made the choice to act out. It puts the child and the educator on opposite sides of the table, defensively reacting against each other. More often than not, a behavioral health issue is the culprit. The second approach allows the educator to come alongside the child and to put the behavioral health issue or trauma on the other side of the table. When the teachers or support staff come alongside students, the blame is not on the students and their choices but on the life circumstances that caused their pain in the first place. Shifting from the question of what is wrong with these students to what happened to these students gives us a new and more accurate framework for viewing students and the issues and concerns they bring to the classroom every day.

I understand that this isn't always an easy shift for educators to make and that the issues aren't always easy to recognize. A broken arm or heart disease has a clear path to diagnosis, but identifying behavioral health issues is hard. When does sadness become depression? apprehension become anxiety? fear become phobia? Yet in the last few decades, trauma, anxiety, depression, and other correlating issues have skyrocketed in our schools. These major underlying stressors are no longer affecting only a few students—they are having an impact on *many* of our students.

EXPERT IM

Our teachers are on the front lines. A teacher is usually the first person who recognizes that something is off with a student. If a student shuts down, how does the teacher handle that? Do they know the right questions to ask? We want everybody to have a common language.

—Dr. Brad Breedlove
Chief academic officer of Union County Public Schools, North Carolina

To better understand behavioral health issues, think of them on a continuum. The first point on the continuum is *development.* As students develop and grow, there are opportunities to help them learn the kinds of SEL skills that will give them a healthy foundation in school and in life. The next point is *prevention.* If those skills are not incorporated early enough, catching students in the prevention stage might take more time, energy, intentionality, and focus, but doing so can often stave off more serious issues. By the time students reach the next point on the continuum, *intervention*, the stakes are much higher. Intervening in students' behavioral and mental health can be difficult and complicated. The final point, *treatment*, is the riskiest of all. If students need treatment for their issues, their lives and futures can hang in the balance. Figure 3.1 illustrates this continuum and where most schools are spending their time and resources. Figure 3.2 shows where we *should* be spending our time and resources to both improve student well-being and better prepare them for the future.

No one who works with and cares about students wants to wait until things reach the riskiest stage. If it's possible to save even some students

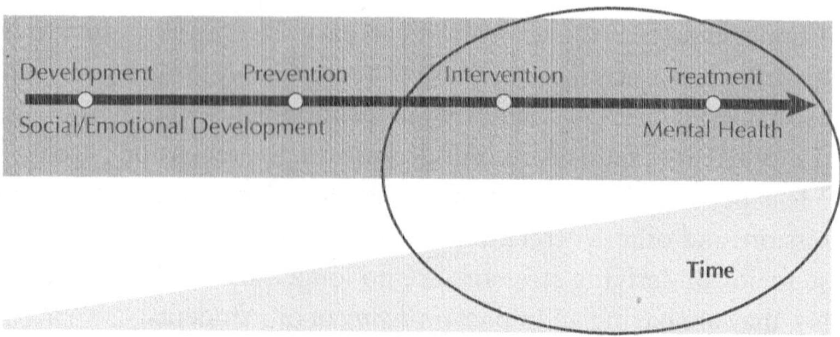

FIGURE 3.1 The Behavioral Health Continuum: Where We Are

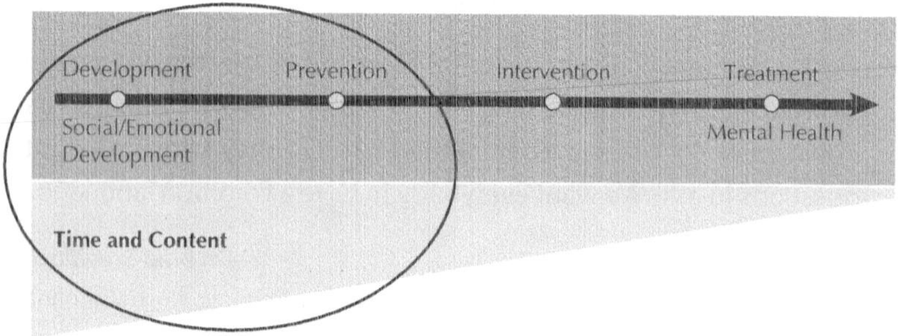

FIGURE 3.2 The Behavioral Health Continuum: Where We Need to Be

from getting to the point where they need intervention and treatment, incorporating effective SEL at the development stage just makes sense.

Yet far too many schools wait until the intervention and treatment stages to address SEL issues. As students struggle with behavioral health issues, we pull them out of the classroom and engage a growing "support staff" to attempt to address the students' issues and challenges. This enables the core academic teachers to get on with academic preparation. It's a little like waiting until high school to teach someone to read. If that happened, people would say the system failed the student. In the same way, we should teach SEL with the ABCs, so that by the time students graduate, they have the academic and social and emotional skills to succeed in life. And success in life is a goal that we as educators all share.

A question we all need to consider: Is it our job to develop core academic skills in our students, or is our job broader than that? Is it the development of the whole child? Today, with changes to student life and to our world, it's the latter. We're now responsible for developing both academics and behavioral health skills and knowledge. To do so, we need to start implementing realistic, easily employed initiatives that offer teachers the flexibility required in diverse classrooms.

Flexible Strategies, Not Rigid Initiatives

SEL is not based on fuzzy, pie-in-the sky, idealistic concepts. Successful strategies and concrete procedures for addressing this critical challenge have now been developed by some of our nation's most innovative districts. A 2017 study of the nation's most rapidly improving schools and districts, conducted by the American Association of School Administrators, the International Center for Leadership in Education, and the Successful Practices Network,[5] demonstrated the need for school leaders to

- Recognize that behavioral health lies on the continuum from development to prevention to intervention to treatment and that more support is needed on the lower end as a preemptive measure.
- See ensuring behavioral development and health as a core responsibility of our schools, not simply a support system for select students.
- Use a framework to guide initiative development, curriculum, instructional strategies, and professional learning for all staff.

These three needs fit with what we've already learned in this chapter and point to the critical mindset shift that school administrators and educators must undergo as they set the vision for their schools' curricula. But how we implement these changes is just as important as why.

EXPERT IM

Teaching children to control their own behavior is just as important as A, B, C and one, two, three. We need to start laying the groundwork early so that students can be successful all the way through school. By the time students get to the later grades, teachers are seeing serious issues with their level of regulation.

—Jaime Bonczyk
Executive director, Hopkins Early Learning Center

Okay, okay, I can hear it now. Some of you are probably groaning at the idea of one more big idea to focus on in an already overly packed school day. But I have good news: implementing effective SEL is not simply "adding one more thing" to educators' already overflowing responsibilities. Instead, these are strategies that are responsive to the ever-changing and real-time needs of students. These aren't rigid strategies that teachers need to pile on top of their other binders full of standards, rules, and methodologies. These are flexible strategies that will make work easier—not harder—for teachers every single day.

Integrating SEL: What the Research Tells Us

Not everyone implements SEL the way we at ICLE have found to be the most effective. And that's okay. We believe it's a positive sign that many in the field are attempting to design SEL curricula for schools. This indicates that the industry grasps the urgency in supporting SEL and its growing importance to the world beyond school. Schools are taking an important first step toward positive change in education. What we're learning at ICLE, however, is that many of these initiatives are often inflexible and generic. They lack the flexibility to meet the needs of individual students. The initiatives are also too often divorced from academic learning, which results in the missed opportunity to capitalize on the augmented learning that occurs when all three parts of the brain work together.

The latest research shows that for SEL to generate the greatest benefit, three features need to be in place.[6] SEL should

1. Incorporate social-emotional skills in a specific order based on when students are developmentally ready for them.
2. Be flexible and depend on easy-to-apply strategies, not a full curriculum. We call these "kernels," as they are small but powerful SEL opportunities that can be sprinkled throughout the day at teachable moments to help students grow a range of social and emotional skills.
3. Be responsive to individual student needs in real time. If SEL is truly taking place in real time, it will do so not just in the classroom but also anywhere a need for SEL kernels arises—the cafeteria, the sports field, hallways, the school bus, and so on. This means that SEL must be the responsibility of every adult in and around schools.

When built on these three features of successful SEL, initiatives optimize the interplay between all three parts of the brain. They address and enhance the way students feel about themselves as learners. This kind of SEL implementation is also integrated into the full school learning environment. And, as good teaching should do, this approach keeps the focus on the students more than on the content.

Meeting You Where You Are

To incorporate the three features of successful SEL, we at ICLE have been committed to developing a plan that can support schools through the strategic implementation of evidence-backed SEL opportunities. With neuroscience, learning relationships, and SEL research in mind, we have designed an integrated approach that supports whole-brain and whole-child development.

To address SEL and behavioral health challenges, schools and districts must do the following:

- **Define the problem.** Using survey instruments and discussion/focus groups representing district teachers, administrators, parents, and community members, work to clearly identify the challenges within the district. Districts need to "own the issue" and not treat it as just a national problem. Through data collection and analysis, districts can understand the unique nature of the needs in their specific context.
- **Establish district goals.** After defining the problem, create clearly identified and measurable goals and a plan to monitor progress.
- **Create the culture.** Through a series of presentations and discussion sessions both within and across the district—and that pull applicable data—create a culture that will support a comprehensive boardroom-to-classroom plan to address district behavioral health challenges. A key piece of this process will be professional development that supports every adult on campus in fine-tuning his or her own social-emotional skills, addressing individual stressors, and practicing appropriate and effective application of SEL at every moment it's needed.
- **Develop an instructional plan.** Create the scope and sequence for the preK–12 instructional content and strategies to integrate SEL into the

ongoing instructional initiative. Instructional content and strategies from the districts that have been most successful in addressing the issue can be used as your point of departure. This will save your district considerable time and expense. The plan must remain flexible and highly utilitarian—this is not about high-level ideals but precise strategies for specific classrooms and situations.

- **Address needs for intervention and treatment.** The four previous actions will provide your district with a solid plan to address SEL at the development and prevention stages. Unfortunately, you will still have some children in crisis who will need intervention and treatment. Fortunately, our experience is showing that the number of children needing this level of support will decline dramatically with a solid development and prevention plan. However, you must still have a plan that includes the best strategies and procedures to assist these students in crisis.

This approach of beginning with data collection, making a specific plan for each school, focusing first on educator training, and then implementing SEL throughout the school curriculum ensures that SEL is delivered to all students, not just those with overt mental health issues. As we examined earlier, waiting to think about SEL until students are in need of intervention and treatment is a shortsighted, harmful strategy. By contrast, the ICLE approach to incorporating SEL improves learning outcomes for students, better prepares them for our uncertain future, and helps prevent mental health issues from developing or worsening. As a result, resources are freed up to deliver more targeted, timely support and interventions to students who need them most. This is a huge benefit for districts, schools, educators, students, and parents.

A Model to Guide Us

CASEL has designed a practical rubric that helps districts from beginning to end in incorporating SEL effectively in schools. For the entire rubric—including comprehensive, step-by-step directions for implementing and evaluating an SEL initiative—please see https://casel.org/wp-content/uploads/2016/09/Theory-of-Action-CDI-District-Rubric.pdf.

The rubric will help districts through the readiness phase, the planning phase, and the implementation phase and give them the necessary tools to create a sustainable SEL initiative. This is a comprehensive approach to providing SEL opportunities to all students throughout a district or school. But when it comes to specific interventions, teachers need the flexibility and freedom to select strategies that best fit the diverse needs of their students and classrooms.

Immediate Interventions: SEL Kernels

Currently being designed by Stephanie M. Jones, a professor at the Harvard Graduate School of Education, and researchers from the Harvard Graduate School of Education, "kernels" are simple but effective techniques that teachers can easily use and adapt to meet their needs. Jones is also the director of the Ecological Approaches to Social and Emotional Learning (EASEL) lab and a thought leader for ICLE. In recent years, she has been conducting pioneering research focused on the impact of SEL interventions on behavioral and academic outcomes and classroom practices in preschool and elementary school.

The kernels that Jones and her team are developing are bite-sized strategies that promote specific, positive behavior changes. They're called kernels because they're easily implemented, self-contained practices that can be selected to fit the learning styles, skill levels, interests, and goals of any K–6 classroom in any school. Easily integrated, these kernels will align with the basic structure of the following three sample activities:[7]

- Turtle technique for calming down
  - **Description:** using a turtle metaphor, the child holds self, breathes through nose, and engages in verbal or subverbal self-coaching to calm down
  - **SEL domain:** managing emotions and behavior
  - **Behaviors affected:** reduces arousal and aggression against peers or adults
- Nonverbal transition cues
  - **Description:** the teacher uses visual, kinesthetic, and/or auditory cues to signal a need to shift attention or tasks in a specific, patterned way

    - **SEL domain:** cognitive flexibility, attention, and understanding social cues
    - **Behaviors affected:** reduces dawdling, increases time on task and engaged learning, and gives more time for instruction
- **Peer-to-peer written praise**
    - **Description:** children write praise for peers on a pad, wall display, or photo album (and/or read them aloud)
    - **SEL domain**: prosocial behavior, conflict resolution
    - **Behaviors affected:** increases social competence, academic achievement, and physical health; reduces violence, aggression, and vandalism

Jones's team will curate a set of the most promising SEL strategies currently being used in evidence-based initiatives and offer them to schools. Schools will then be able to choose from among these kernel-sized strategies based on their needs, and Jones and her team will provide training and technical assistance to launch the strategies into practice and then evaluate the outcome.

To help with application, each kernel will be presented in a flash-card format, with the "what," "why," and "how" of the intervention on one side and "Tips for Success," directions for debriefing, and guidelines for continued learning on the other side. If you'd like to learn more about the release of the kernels, be sure to check the following: https://easel.gse.harvard.edu. Also, if you'd like additional guidance on how to create a culture that supports the behavioral health of all students, please contact us at ICLE for more information on SEL and effective SEL practices.

From both a personal and professional perspective, nearly all of us have struggled with how to help the children we interact with every day to cope with stress in their lives. As with all issues related to physical and mental health, early intervention is very important. SEL needs to be a central part of that early intervention for all our children. We have a responsibility to develop the whole child—not just the "academic" child. It's time to love the whole child and to do everything we can to help children develop life's most critical skills—skills that will help them thrive both now and in the future. As we'll see in the next chapter, one key to doing so is to cultivate strong, compassionate connections between staff and students.

LESSONS FOR THE FUTURE

- SEL is key to giving students the basic skills they can learn over time to develop self-awareness, self-management, social awareness, relationship skills, and responsible decision-making. These skills are vital to success in school, the workplace, and society.
- We know that understanding where students are coming from, how the brain develops, and the underlying causes of their behavior can help teachers come alongside them in a way that increases students' ability to connect and learn well, which is beneficial to the students, the educators, and the schools.
- SEL is not new but rather is based on the kind of instinctive strategies good teachers have always used. Defining the SEL skills and competencies will enable educators to ready students for the kind of complex thinking and emotional health they need to thrive.
- Successful SEL initiatives in schools begin with developmental and prevention skills, rather than waiting for the intervention and treatment stages.
- SEL initiatives are not rigid, but instead employ strategies that enable educators to respond to anything that comes up in real time; these strategies are incorporated throughout the entire curriculum to help students achieve the most benefits emotionally, socially, and academically.
- In order to effectively implement SEL initiatives across curricula, schools and districts must define the problem, establish district goals, create the culture, develop an instructional plan, and address needs for intervention and treatment.

4

Rigor and Relevance: It Now Starts with Relationships

For years, we at the International Center for Leadership in Education (ICLE) have been talking about "the third R"—relationships—as a key step toward relevance and rigor. As many of the changes and challenges presented in the first three chapters of the book took shape, we began discussing the importance of relationships more frequently and more passionately. Collaborating with educators to increase rigor and relevance, we emphasized the importance of forming trusting relationships with all their students. At the same time, we saw that meaningful relationships catalyzed greater relevance and more rigor in the classroom. We could see again and again the power of relationships to develop resilience and persistence, encourage students to go deeper with their learning, and contribute to their self-confidence and belief in their own potential.

More recently, we've watched as many students—some surprisingly young—face serious mental health issues. Because of this, we've started banging the drum of relationships louder still. We've included in the conversation the importance of SEL, discussed in depth in the previous chapter, as both a conduit for and outcome of high-quality relationships. We know that when children are suffering with anxiety, depression, or low self-worth, it's incredibly hard for them to begin to climb out of it if they feel uncared for and unseen by the adults in their lives. This means that the need for meaningful relationships in schools has grown only more critical—and for reasons that clearly extend beyond rigor and relevance. Yes, relationships are the foundation on which greater relevance and increased rigor are built. But further, today and in the future, relationships are critical to our students' well-being and their capacity to engage with learning and excel in school. This is why relationships are no longer just a key step toward rigor and relevance; they're now the *first* step toward rigor and relevance. The third R has become the first R.

All of us know that relationships in schools are powerful. We know this intuitively. And we know this from experience. Yet only recently has research begun to catch up with what we believe.[1] This not only validates our collective hunch that we must devote significant effort to cultivating relationships with all our students but also begins to show us why and how. In this chapter, I'll explain the what, why, and how of building learning relationships in schools. This includes providing a number of strategies for developing positive, high-quality relationships with students both in the classroom and throughout the school building. Before we dive into these specifics, however, let's review the ICLE Rigor/Relevance Framework and look at how it has evolved to accommodate the growing importance of relationships.

The Three R's

In 1991, I created the Application Model, which comprises the following five levels:

1. Knowledge in one discipline
2. Apply in discipline
3. Apply across disciplines
4. Apply to real-world predictable situations
5. Apply to real-world unpredictable situations

I then merged the Application Model with Bloom's Taxonomy to create the Rigor/Relevance Framework. The framework thus integrated Bloom's increasingly complex level of thinking with increasingly complex levels of relevant application. The result is a framework with four quadrants representing possible combinations of rigor and relevance. The Rigor/Relevance Framework was designed as a simple—yet robust—tool to help educators plan for and assess higher levels of rigor and relevance in the classroom. Figure 4.1 illustrates the framework.

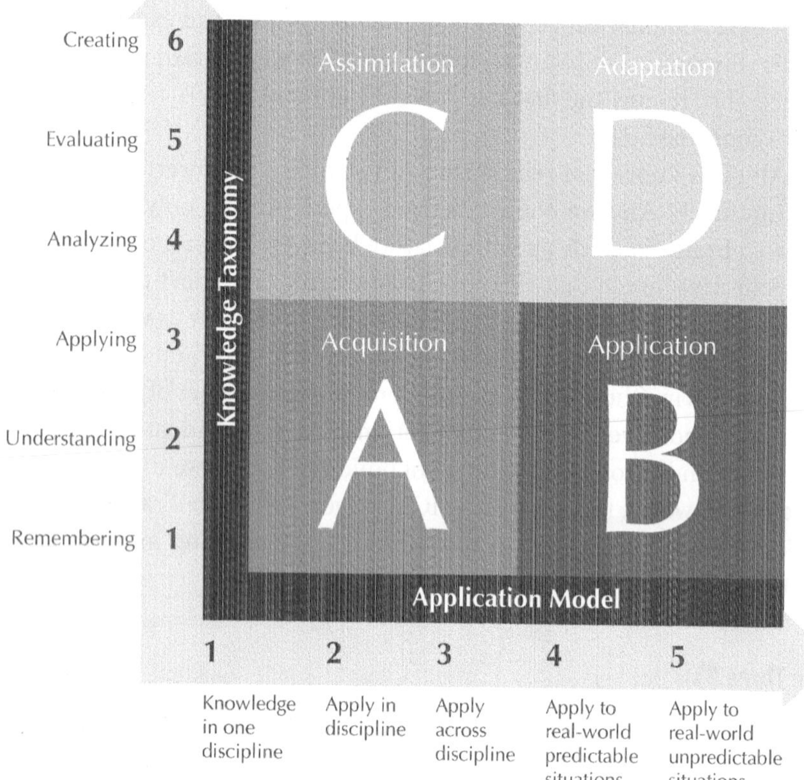

FIGURE 4.1 The Rigor/Relevance Framework

As you can see, the framework has four quadrants. Quadrant A represents simple recall and basic understanding of knowledge for its own sake. Quadrant C represents more complex thinking, as well as knowledge for its own sake. Examples of Quadrant A thinking include knowing how many planets are in our solar system and that Abraham Lincoln wrote the Gettysburg Address. Quadrant C embraces higher levels of knowledge, such as knowing how the US system of government works and analyzing the benefits of diversity in our country.

Quadrants B and D represent action or high degrees of application. Quadrant B includes knowing how to use math skills to count change from a purchase. The ability to access information in wide-area network systems and the ability to gather knowledge from a variety of sources to solve a complex problem in the workplace are types of Quadrant D knowledge. More succinctly, think of it this way: Quadrant A is acquisition, Quadrant B is application, Quadrant C is assimilation, and Quadrant D is adaptation.

Intended as a practical model for designing instruction and assessment, the framework is based on the following premises:

- Teaching in the twenty-first century has to be more than just transmitting facts or routine skills; facts are available online, and routine skills can be performed by any phone, tablet, laptop, or desktop computer.
- Meaningful and lasting learning is an active process, not "sit 'n' git."
- Learning is no longer just about knowing. Instead, it's now more about solving problems that have no obvious solution.
- Being able to apply knowledge is more important than simply comprehending it.
- Higher levels of real-world application provide access to higher levels of academic knowledge and achievement.

Over the years, we at ICLE have had a common refrain: relevance makes rigor possible, and rigor makes life success possible. That is, by making the work we ask our students to do relevant to their lives and their interests, they'll engage in more rigorous thinking and learning tasks. If the work feels irrelevant to them, they'll often be unwilling to engage or pursue meaningful levels of rigor.

As we guided more and more educators in the use of the Rigor/Relevance Framework, it became clear that positive, high-quality relationships make relevance possible. These are relationships characterized by connection, support, and a true sense of caring. In other words, the framework achieves its greatest potential when it's encompassed by these types of meaningful relationships. If a teacher wants to make learning relevant—and who in our profession doesn't—then she or he has to know what individual students find interesting, fun, and engaging. To gain this knowledge, teachers must earn their students' trust so that the students, in turn, open up, share their lives, discuss their interests, and reveal their goals.

This is made possible only through relationships.

Figure 4.2 shows how we've added relationships to the Rigor/Relevance Framework to create a new model that we call the Relationships Framework.

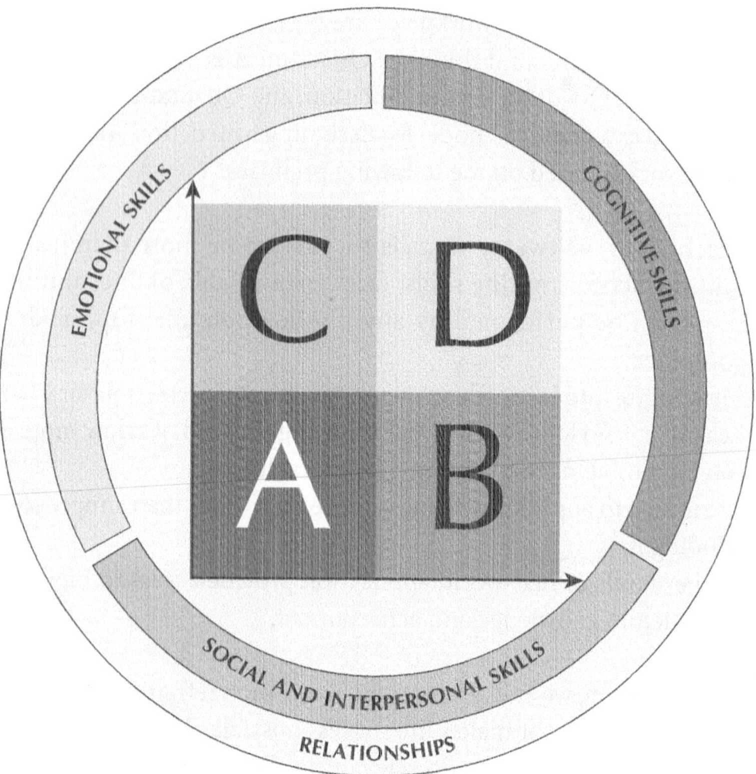

FIGURE 4.2 The Relationships Framework

This framework better represents the true association between the three R's: Relationships → Relevance → Rigor.

Yes, relevance still makes rigor possible. But, as many of us have learned in schools and classrooms across the country, what's relevant to one student isn't necessarily relevant to another. Relationships help us individualize relevance. Relationships help build the skills—the emotional skills, the social and interpersonal skills, and the cognitive skills—that students need today and will need in the future to confront a rapidly changing world.

Stronger Relationships, Deeper Learning

For many students, school is often a place where relationships are established and nurtured. These relationships can be with classmates, teammates, administrators, support staff, or other adults in the school, but teachers are the school's primary point of daily contact for students. And as we've seen in the first few chapters of this book, today's students are fundamentally different from those of the past. As children of the twenty-first century, they're accustomed to being actively engaged with technology, which has conditioned them to expect experiences that are personalized, that are often collaborative, and that offer immediate feedback. Without such personalization and instant connectivity, they tend to become disengaged. This is a serious problem—disengaged students may be memorizing facts and following rules, but they're not learning. More to the point, they're not learning how to learn.

Relevance alleviates this problem. Relevance helps students learn most effectively and take responsibility for their own learning through the following benefits:

- They see a reason to learn.
- They can relate what they are learning to their lives outside school.
- They're actively engaged in learning and are not viewed as passive or empty receptacles into which knowledge must be packed.
- They receive instruction that takes into account their interests and learning style.
- They feel safe, secure, and accepted at school; school is "a good place to be."

For school leaders, therefore, it's imperative to prioritize helping students have the types of positive and supportive school-based relationships—both with adults and with other students—that facilitate relevance. This includes enabling teachers to get to know all students' interests and circumstances, as well as supporting students in cultivating healthy and appropriate relationships that sustain their overall well-being and mental health. In particular, there are two components of high-quality relationships that catalyze relevance: the development of intrinsic motivation and the creation of acceptance, trust, and a sense of belonging. Let's take a closer look at each of these components and examine how they align with psychology and education research.

Passion Makes Motivation

A big mistake that many of us as educators make is to confuse obedience with motivation. It's important to keep in mind that following the rules isn't the same as willfully and passionately tackling a subject or solving a problem. Children and adults alike do their best work when they (or we) *want* to do it. Subsequently, that work, that lesson, or that problem needs to have relevance. And, of course, what's relevant to one child isn't necessarily relevant to another. Any single instructional approach, specific illustrative example, or particular learning app may motivate some students, but fail to engage and motivate the students sitting right beside them. The real danger is the other students may appear to be engaged when they really aren't, lulling teachers into a false sense of satisfaction. The students may only be acting obediently and compliantly, giving the teacher the benefit of the doubt. But in truth, they're not deeply engaged in their own learning. They're not relating. They're not connecting.

This connection is vital. When students find a passion—whether it's sports, horses, cars, or science fiction—it gives them something to engage with, to connect to, and to relate to in their young lives. This motivates them to learn both inside and outside school. The world, rather than just the classroom, becomes a place of learning and exploration. Instead of being driven by extrinsic motivation, which stems from rewards or punishment, students begin to discover an intrinsic motivation. And this special interest becomes a connection point for developing relationships with teachers, classmates, and new and old friends. As Ray McNulty, a current senior fellow at ICLE and president of the Successful Practices Network, explains:

> Education is personal. A school valedictorian needs to be good at everything. But what about the student who is great at art? or music? or poetry? The student who is passionate about one aspect of school? Often, they don't feel good about it because it's not rewarded in the same way as achievement across all topics. It's not respected in the same way. But we should be honoring individual expertise. Having a focused passion shows the ability to learn deeply. It's very powerful. And if we as educators can tap into that passion, learning takes on a whole new relevance.

Connecting with and relating to people, to ideas, and to things creates engagement, an essential condition for learning. The nation's most rapidly improving schools understand and act on this important concept. In my study of these schools, a key practice I noted was the active relationship building that took place between teachers and students. School cultures that emphasized and nurtured relationships had a powerful impact on student achievement and success. I know from experience that connecting with and then building a relationship with every student in every class would be a difficult task for even the most committed teachers. What is essential, however, is that each and every student have a relationship with at least one adult in your school—someone who knows the student well, understands what motivates him or her, and cares about the student as an individual.

Acceptance, Trust, and Student Well-Being

Psychologists and sociologists tell us that supportive social relationships are *emotionally sustaining*, meaning that they enhance mental and physical health. In addition, supportive relationships provide a sense of *personal control*, which is defined as belief that we can control, or at least influence, our lives through personal decisions and actions.[2] This is true of everyone, but is even more important for young people, who are still developing their own identities and finding their place in the world. Teens may be the most needful of these positive relationships.

EXPERT IM

If a child doesn't feel engaged and that they belong, they're not going to be as successful at learning. So if you look into the future, what we as adults need to do is to ensure that kids feel connected, feel like they belong. And where is the one place we can ensure that for every child? School.

—Shauna McDonald
Executive director, Playworks Minnesota

When kids feel that they are accepted for who they are, they're more likely to be accepting of others. Another important outcome of relationships is the building of trust. Trust matters for students, of course, because it creates a sense of security, increased confidence, and the feeling that someone else cares about their well-being and success. In addition, students who feel they have good relationships with both their teachers and peers experience a greater sense of belonging in school, which results in greater motivation to become engaged learners. All of these feelings—acceptance, trust, and belonging—are derived from care and safety when students believe that teachers and peers see them as valuable; in turn, these students develop critical social and emotional skills that are further reinforced through caring relationships. And, just as important, they begin building a strong sense of what psychologists call *self-efficacy.*

First popularized by Albert Bandura, a psychology professor at Stanford University, self-efficacy is defined as confidence in one's own ability to develop strategies and complete tasks necessary to be successful in various activities. More simply put, self-efficacy is an individual's belief in her or his capabilities. This includes the belief in one's ability to perform specific tasks, including solving a problem, writing a paper, taking a test, giving a speech, or even starting a business. Clearly, a high level of self-efficacy is beneficial: unless we truly believe we can produce the results we want, we have little incentive to persevere in the face of challenges.

Over the past few decades, dozens of studies have examined the importance of self-efficacy in academics and career success. Multiple cross-sectional and longitudinal studies have found a positive influence of a high sense of self-efficacy on salary, job satisfaction, and career success. The tenets of self-efficacy have been tested, studied, and verified in a variety of settings and disciplines, including the study of social skills, assertiveness, depression, athletic performance, and overall health.[3]

Bandura and others have found that our sense of self-efficacy plays a major positive role in how we approach goals and challenges. People with a strong sense of self-efficacy view challenging problems as tasks to be mastered. They develop a deeper interest in the activities in which they participate and form a stronger sense of commitment to their interests. They also recover quickly from setbacks and disappointment. People with a weak sense of self-efficacy, by contrast, avoid challenging tasks. They believe that difficult tasks and situations are beyond their capabilities and exhibit a tendency to focus on personal failings and negative outcomes. This causes them to quickly lose confidence in their abilities. It's an understatement to say that this can be detrimental. Self-efficacy affects nearly every aspect of life—how well we learn, work, and live.

So how can we as educators help increase students' self-efficacy? This is where relationships come in: there's a motivational power in language.

According to Bandura's research, we can be led, through verbal suggestion, into believing that we can cope successfully with a challenge that has overwhelmed us in the past. That is, when we're persuaded that we possess the capabilities to master difficult situations, we'll apply greater effort to these challenges than we otherwise would. Bandura notes, "Persuasive boosts in perceived self-efficacy lead people to try hard enough to succeed; they promote development of skills and a sense of personal efficacy." By contrast, Bandura found that negative feedback can exacerbate an already fragile sense of self-efficacy. To break what he called "exacerbation cycles" of people with low self-efficacy, Bandura suggests that we should avoid negatively reinforcing a skill deficiency, or promoting the idea that a particular task is easy.[4]

This just reaffirms a point we all already know: words matter. And by extension, relationships matter—a lot.

Although there's plenty of research to support the effectiveness in education of developing strong, supportive relationships, what do the numbers actually tell us? Is there objective data that supports the contention that relationships are truly the first R in developing rigor and relevance?

The Quantitative Basis

John Hattie is an education researcher whom I have great respect for, and I use his research to guide much of our work at ICLE. Hattie, a professor of education at Melbourne University in Australia, undertook the largest-ever quantitative research study of the effect of different factors on educational outcomes. This study included the synthesis of findings from fourteen hundred meta-analyses of eighty thousand studies involving 300 million students.[5] Yes, you read that right—300 million students.

In the study, he measured the influence of 256 educational factors in terms of effect size. The average effect size for all the interventions he studied was 0.40. (The higher the number, the more effective the intervention.) Hattie's' meta-analysis lists "teacher-student relationships" as among the most effective influences on student achievement, with an effect size of 0.72, higher than "professional development" (0.62), "teaching strategies" (0.60), or student "socio-economic status" (0.57). Hattie said of relationships: "It is teachers who have created positive teacher-student relationships that are more likely to have the above average effects on student achievement." More amazing, Hattie found a high level of self-efficacy, a result of good-quality relationships, to have an effect size of 0.92, higher than nearly all of the other 255 influences that were tracked. The message is clear: if every educator in a school is purposefully creating moments that reinforce learning relationships, then the school is working to enhance all students' learning potential and well-being.

All of this supports a clear reality of education today and in the future: teachers must see themselves as facilitators of the learning process, not merely as disseminators of knowledge. This understanding represents a major shift in expertise from how most teachers were trained and from what has been expected of them in the past. Being the voice at the front of the classroom will no longer be sufficient. Instead, supportive, high-quality pedagogy and methodology based on knowledge of individual student interests or passions will define the highest levels of teaching performance. In the age of search, algorithms, and artificial intelligence, building positive, supportive relationships with students will be more critical than ever and will trump a teacher's content expertise.

Building Learning Relationships

Making these changes won't be easy. But it must be done. The transition will require support from leadership, a significant amount of time, and training for many teachers. Primarily, however, the shift will require educators to understand and adopt a new vision of relationship-based student learning. This new type of learning incorporates the following changes:

- Rules are negotiated, not mandated.
- Authority exists with respect, rather than without question.
- Students are actively engaged, instead of passive and quiet.
- Risk-taking is encouraged, not discouraged.
- Failure is seen as a valuable learning experience.
- Meaningful and high-impact formative assessment of student progress is understood and embraced by students, teachers, administrators, and parents.
- Positive reinforcement and rewards are used, instead of negative feedback and punishment.
- Teachers guide learning and give encouragement, rather than simply disseminate knowledge.

In all fairness, these are practices that many teachers already follow, especially special education teachers; teachers of the gifted and talented; career and technical education teachers; fine arts teachers; coaches and physical education and health teachers; and counselors, student services providers, tutors, and advisors. All of these roles as educators afford distinctive opportunities to build relationships and interact closely with students. Further, all of these roles and teaching specializations illustrate the important connection between relationships and learning. In building learning relationships, all teachers of all subjects must understand and apply the consistent approaches in their everyday activities and student interactions. The teachers who are most successful at building relationships are the ones who

- Know their students' academic histories.
- Make efforts to recognize and then tap into individual student needs and learning styles.
- Make respectful efforts to try to know something personal about every student they teach.
- Build relationships with their students by showing caring concern for their academic and personal well-being.
- Volunteer for duties that put them in contact with students and families in situations outside the classroom—for example, coaching, advising, chaperoning, mentoring.
- Converse with students informally, listen, share personal anecdotes, acknowledge students' academic and extracurricular achievements, and generally demonstrate that they are approachable as caring and trustworthy adults.
- Let their personality, sense of humor, perspective, compassion, and humanity show through while maintaining the necessary professional distance and avoiding trying to become a "pal."
- Nurture relationships with colleagues, parents, and the community.

Because teachers have the most regular contact with students, they have the greatest opportunity—and responsibility—to establish positive relationships with students. When teachers are successful, school variables such as attendance, dropout rate, educational continuance, extracurricular participation, behavioral issues, and school culture as a whole tend to improve. Those variables, in turn, contribute directly to student achievement and future success, the ultimate goal for all of us in education.

EXPERT IM

Technology definitely changes our experiences. Some things are amplified; some things are reduced. But what makes us uniquely human are the kinds of interactions we have. The relationships that we nurture within schools, within families, and within communities will directly determine our collective success.

—Karen Cator
President and CEO, Digital Promise

For a true culture of learning relationships to take hold, however, supportive relationships must also exist among the adults in the building. This should include all classified staff—lunchroom monitors, bus drivers, librarians, specialists, and so on. Learning relationships are the concern of every adult on campus, and every adult on campus must understand why relationships are so critical and what their role is in reinforcing them. In terms of leadership strategy, this means that every adult on campus needs professional development and support to help improve his or her skills in building learning relationships.

Students can also be "teachers" and relationship builders within a school. Many schools use senior students to advise, tutor, and coach other students to enhance learning. Some students tutor or coach younger children. Others serve as peer mentors. Some schools even have student volunteers on "mediation panels" to help address behavioral issues or settle disputes. Therefore, although it's easy to put the onus on teachers to create meaningful relationships within schools, the reality is that the process needs to become part of the broader school culture. To help with this goal, my colleagues at ICLE, Harvard professor Stephanie Jones, and I have worked together to create a Relationship Rubric that offers a model for developing the types of relationships that lead to relevance and rigor.

The Relationship Rubric

Simply put, the Relationships Rubric is a leading-edge framework for planning and observing positive relationships in the classroom. Unfortunately, easily applied research around teacher–student relationships is limited and can be challenging because of the often intangible, squishy nature of relationships. To build the rubric, we reviewed available research, observed the strategies used in our nation's most rapidly improving schools, and relied on what we know to be true about human connection and helping students feel seen, understood, valued, and cared for. Ultimately, we distilled the core components of building and nurturing relationships in the classroom down to three indicators: vulnerability, connection, and compassion.

Vulnerability

Vulnerability is probably the most opaque indicator, yet the most important. University of Houston professor and best-selling author Brené Brown, a renowned researcher on the topics of courage and empathy, among others, is leading a shift in how we perceive vulnerability. Although vulnerability has historically been thought of as a negative state, her research shows that "it's the most accurate way to measure courage" and is a powerful pathway to openness and growth. Brown defines vulnerability as "uncertainty, risk, and emotional exposure." Vulnerability asks us to experience and face all the emotions that come with risk-taking—both the positive ones that come with success and the negative ones that come with failure. The flip side of this is growth, resilience, and unconditional self-worth. In facing and processing emotions—rather than avoiding them—we can prevent them from festering and escalating to a point of self-harm or harm to others.

The healthiest relationships, including in the classroom, are those in which both parties feel safe being vulnerable. There are two primary goals of helping students become comfortable with vulnerability. The first is to help them develop positive self-perceptions as learners through an openness to healthy risk-taking and the capacity to persevere regardless of outcome (think self-efficacy). The second is to help them redefine having and facing emotions as a courageous act of strength, not a sad sign of weakness. In the classroom, fostering an empowered understanding of vulnerability involves

- Teaching students that learning is courageously vulnerable and presents typical highs (joy, satisfaction, curiosity, etc.) and lows (frustration, confusion, productive struggle, etc.)
- Using the language of learning (e.g., growth mindset language as explained in Carol Dweck's book *Mindset: The New Psychology of*

Success), engaging students in a dialogue about their emotional experiences as they learn, grow, or confront and overcome setbacks so that emotions are normalized and validated

- Reframing perceived setbacks and failures as normal and as opportunities to grow and to develop resilience
- The teacher's showing vulnerability by sharing personal stories of setbacks and growth

Connection

The goal of connecting with students is to establish trust. As mentioned earlier in the chapter, without trust, we can't have relationships. Research shows that trust is a by-product of teachers' connecting with students not just academically but also personally. This includes learning students' interests, developing cultural competence and understanding students' cultures and home lives, and engaging with students' families. This kind of connection sheds light on students' strengths and weaknesses. In the classroom, developing this type of connection requires that

- The teacher makes a regular and concerted effort to get to know students on a personal level.
- Students see their interests, passions, culture, and personal and family lives as relevant to learning and are given opportunities to incorporate them into learning tasks.
- As a result of knowing students' weaknesses, the teacher offers scaffolded and personalized support to meet students where they are and address weaknesses.
- Students know their strengths, learn how to leverage them in learning, and feel supported in addressing weaknesses.
- The teacher makes students feel safe and shame-free when they ask for help.

Compassion

When we extend compassion to others, we reject knee-jerk judgments, mitigate bias, and choose to lead with empathy. When teachers are compassionate, they view students as the whole children they are and make students feel seen, heard, and understood.

For teachers to be compassionate, they must be self-aware; they must know their biases and take steps to eliminate them. They must also lead with empathy. This is particularly true in the face of behavioral issues. Compassion can actually help the teacher better understand the root cause of such issues. When students receive compassion, they begin to feel capable of rising above any biased perceptions, self-limiting beliefs, or detrimental behavioral patterns.

Compassion is also a pathway toward reducing disproportionalities and establishing equity in instruction and learning. As brain research shows, this is because, as we explored in chapter 3, *all* learning is tied to SEL. Instruction that works to reduce negative perceptions of an individual student or certain student demographic groups promotes learning that nurtures social and emotional development and compassion for others. In the classroom, fostering compassion requires the following:

- Instead of reflexively taking punitive measures when a student misbehaves, the teacher tries to understand the root cause of the behavior. Instead of approaching the student's actions from a "What's wrong with them?" mindset, the teacher adopts one of "What happened to them?" The goal is to avoid labeling the student negatively and help the student create a new, positive behavioral pattern.
- The teacher has a range of flexible SEL instructional strategies to help defuse tension and behavioral problems and help students reduce stress in real time.
- Students have strategies to self-regulate behavior and help themselves and peers reduce stress.
- Students demonstrate compassion for their classmates.

This sounds like a lot to understand and implement, I know. So to help you build your own culture of learning relationships more quickly and effectively, we at ICLE have developed a detailed rubric that illustrates four levels of success—Beginning, Emerging, Developed, and Well Developed—in implementing vulnerability, connection, and compassion in the classroom. To see and download the rubric, go to www.leadered.com/relationshipsrubric.

Much of the process and effort in building supportive relationships focuses on teachers and how they manage their classrooms, but there's still a clear need for strong, dedicated leadership. Be aware, though, that this is not the school leader as top-down dictator or drill sergeant. Rather, creating a school-wide atmosphere that promotes learning relationships requires a leader who is capable of transforming a school environment so that students *and* teachers can flourish and grow together.

The Leader's Role

Although teachers have the most direct impact on student relationships, don't underestimate your role—or the role of any other leader—in developing a culture that supports the types of learning relationships that undergird the Rigor/Relevance Framework. Leaders must take responsibility for promoting constructive relationships across the entire school and district. For example, leaders must select, support, and evaluate teachers with an explicit consideration of their ability to build strong relationships with students. If this type of relationship building is not discussed and valued, it won't happen.

Schools can be student-friendly or not. School leaders can promote relationships or choose not to develop a culture that recognizes just how critical relationships are to the education process. They can articulate ideas behind developing relationships, yet fail to support those ideas with actions. But, as should be clear by now, students are more likely to make a commitment to engage in rigorous learning when they know that their teachers, parents, and even other students care about how well they do. They're willing to continue making the investment in learning when they feel encouraged, appreciated, and valued. Building good relationships creates relevance, which leads to rigor. It's that simple.

But, as many of us know, simple isn't always easy.

All school leaders need to support teachers in working together—and individually—on improving relationships, regardless of their current level of success. There are many organizational behaviors that foster strong relationships—for example, showing respect, "being there" for students through frequent contact, engaging in active listening, encouraging students to express opinions, avoiding put-downs, using positive humor, talking about cultural relationships, and celebrating student and school accomplishments. These are all keys to creating a culture that nurtures beneficial relationships for students and staff alike. Other supportive **initiatives** that influence relationships in a positive way include the following:

- Mentoring
- Rewards, recognition, and incentives
- Advisory programs
- Partnerships with the business community
- Service learning and community service
- Extracurricular and cocurricular activities
- Family-based activities
- Sports

All of these initiatives help build relationships that acknowledge passion; increase student motivation; improve self-efficacy; and support cultural awareness, respect, tolerance, and understanding. Supportive **structures** such as the following make it easier to develop positive relationships that contribute to learning:

- Community schools
- Small learning communities
- Looping
- Team teaching
- Professional learning communities
- Career and technical education and arts programs

Strong, supportive teacher–student relationships are not a silver bullet that prevents all of today's problems—anxiety, family issues, trauma, or any other negative factors in school. But relationships are perhaps the single most effective remedy, as well as preventive medicine, for many of these challenges. This is especially true if you can employ the first supportive structure named in the previous list by engaging the entire community in developing and nurturing positive learning relationships.

It Takes a Community

Community schools is a general term that refers to a school's strategic engagement of the broader community for the ultimate benefit of students and families. The goal of a community school is to expand or create services that support students' academic achievement, address students' physical and mental health, and offer broader and more convenient ways for families to interact with the school. To reach this goal, the strategy is usually to discover and leverage untapped resources within the community, such as those available through local and state government agencies and services, nonprofit service providers, higher education institutions, philanthropic organizations, and businesses.

For many students, community schools offer the joy of feeling genuinely cared for, not only by the school but by the entire community. This joy includes the freedom that students feel when impediments to their ability to attend and engage in school are lifted. It's the enthusiasm about school that students discover when their physical and mental health needs are met. It's also the motivation educators feel when their leaders leverage community resources so that they can be more effective and their students more engaged in the classroom. For community members, there's a special sense of accomplishment that comes with working for or partnering with a school that has found ways to support all families and make them feel welcome and wanted on campus. Altogether, it creates the pride, care, and sense of ownership that everyone—educators, students, families, and community members—feels for the school.

When the day is done, community schools are about meeting student needs—more of them and more often—to optimize students' capacity to learn. And this just makes sense. Relative to other institutions or services for children, school is where kids spend most of their time. Although students interact with other adults offering services outside school, those adults tend to have only a limited view of their needs. It is the adults at school who get a broader and more whole-child view of students' needs and thus can develop close and trusting relationships with students and their families.

EXPERT IM

It's critical that we as educators think of school as a resource for everyone in the community. When we do, we can provide a focal point for building stronger relationships that truly help students and families be successful.

—MaryEllen Elia
ICLE senior partner and former commissioner of education of the state of New York

When a community school is at its most creative and resourceful, it can contribute to a student's overall well-being and broaden access to ongoing learning and support throughout an entire day, every day. In other words, such a school can influence, to varying degrees, all the components of a student's total health and, thereby, his or her capacity to engage fully in learning. This includes balanced nutrition, access to medical care, access to mental health care, access to rigorous and relevant academic opportunities during and after school hours, a good night's sleep, clean clothes, and supports for parents to help them engage more in their children's learning.

When educators take the accurate view that the school building and its resources do not disappear with the three o'clock release bell, more needs can be met more often. For example, a school in Yonkers, New York, devoted space on its campus for a health clinic for students and their families. The school partnered with a local hospital, which recruited a small team of doctors, nurse practitioners, a psychologist, and a dentist to run the health clinic on the weekends. The hospital paid the providers, and patients visiting the clinic could use Medicaid to cover their expenses.

By operating during the weekends, the clinic enabled students' families to get care (including mental health care) they often had to forgo due to working multiple jobs. At ICLE, we've seen other schools run similar programs on different schedules—one weekday and weeknight plus one weekend day, and so on, based on the particular needs of the community. We've also seen schools partner with state mental health agencies. Sometimes, one of the state psychologists will spend one day every couple of weeks at the school to counsel students. In other cases, where geography is an impediment, a psychologist might Skype with students (in groups or alone) in need of mental health care.

The research on parental involvement in a child's education is unambiguous: children learn more and view themselves as learners when their parents are engaged in their education.[6] Unfortunately, several impediments block too many parents from school engagement. These can range from inconvenient times and location of school meetings, to language barriers, to things more basic, such as embarrassment over a lack of clean clothes. Beyond helping families live with more dignity, health, and comfort, such programs also benefit engagement in two key ways: First, they engender positive feelings toward the school; they cause families to see schools as places that tend not only to children's learning but also to the overall well-being of children and their families. Second, it's not uncommon for families to feel apprehensive or intimidated coming to a school. This is true for many reasons, ranging from their own bad experiences with education to recent unemployment or homelessness. When schools offer practical services to meet basic family needs, families grow more comfortable coming to the campus. Over time, this almost always motivates parents to engage in school and their children's educations in other, more direct ways.

These are just a few of the advantages of community schools in terms of building relationships, including student–teacher relationships, student–student relationships, and school–family relationships. You can learn more about community schools by downloading a detailed study from http://www.leadered.com/pdf/CommunitySchoolsWhitepaper.pdf. The previous explanation, however, should give you a good idea of their power to support students and their well-being. And because of community schools' potential to positively influence nearly every element that improves teaching and learning, they represent organizational leadership and positive relationship building at its best.

I believe that in the face of constantly evolving technology and increasing competition, we need to rethink how we apply rigor and relevance. It can't be yesterday's three R's—relevance creates rigor, and then maybe you need some good relationships. Instead, relationships must come first. Yes, relevance will still get you to rigor. But with the many changes affecting our students, our schools, our world, and how we learn, relevance is nearly impossible to create without first cultivating supportive, high-quality relationships with students. Today and tomorrow, we as educators need to know what matters to children—what motivates them, what concerns them, and what makes them feel connected. Only then can we guide them to true rigor in learning.

LESSONS FOR THE FUTURE

- Teaching in the twenty-first century has to be more than just transmitting facts or routine skills. Relevance makes rigor possible. Relevance and rigor combined lead to success in life. But now we know there's another R that comes *first*: relationships make relevance possible and, in turn, rigor.

- For many students, school is the primary place where relationships are established and nurtured. Teachers are the school's closest point of daily contact, but these relationships can also be with classmates, teammates, administrators, support staff, or other adults in the school. Everyone needs to contribute to building strong learning relationships.
- Positive, high-quality relationships increase intrinsic motivation; create feelings of acceptance, trust, and belonging; improve students' sense of self-efficacy; and help develop social and emotional skills. These are all critical drivers of learning.
- There are three core factors for building and nurturing relationships in the classroom: vulnerability, connection, and compassion. Establishing these factors will help students feel seen, understood, valued, and cared for.
- Although teachers have the most interaction with students, school leaders must actively support the development of positive relationships. They can do this through initiatives such as mentoring, advisory programs, and partnerships, or through such structures as learning communities, teacher continuity, and community schools.

5

Future Focused, Not Forward Focused

Throughout the first eleven months of 1903, most US transportation experts were focused on inventing faster trains that could improve and expand railroad service for the country. For them, making incremental improvements to the current system was the smartest way to meet the transportation needs of a quickly growing country.

Then, in the last month of that year, a couple of brothers from Ohio locked up their bicycle shop and made a journey to North Carolina. On December 17, in Kitty Hawk, they took their Wright Flyer on the first controlled, sustained flight of a powered, heavier-than-air aircraft.

That day, they changed the world of transportation.

The train engineers of the time, dedicated and resourceful as they were, were *forward focused.* They wanted to make an established system as efficient as possible. The Wright brothers were *future focused.* They wanted to transform transportation and take it in a completely new direction—and, in their case, that direction was up!

I'm afraid that many of us in education are entirely too much like those train engineers of the last century. We've inherited an education system that did some amazing things in its day. And we think that by doing some tinkering with standards here or adding a new program or intervention there, we're doing all that can be done to provide the best possible education for the next generation. As long as we're moving forward along the tracks, getting incrementally better at what we did last year, we feel we can credit ourselves with success.

But, as the last few chapters should prove, we can't keep going down the same tracks. With social and technological changes, these tracks are a dead end. Instead, we need to take a step toward the future and *fly.* When we analyze and plan for the changes needed in the twenty-first-century world, we as educators are future focused. We don't seek ways to make things just a little bit better than they already are. We don't hope to squeeze 2 or 3 percent better test scores from an already successful—but outdated—system. We look for innovative solutions that will change the game and deliver a brand-new level of results.

It will never be easy to stand at the edge of the cliff, hoping that all your plans and calculations were right. But the results—the soaring, gravity-defying results—will be well worth it. When we realize that being forward focused is actually a trap, not a solution, we're freed up to plan and implement new approaches that will maximize engagement, increase application, and prepare students for an uncertain, more competitive future.

The Forward-Focus Trap

It's not as if we're making a conscious decision to inch forward instead of lifting our eyes to a new horizon of possibility. Most of our schools *are* moving forward, after all, staying on time and under budget while doing their best to serve students. But as they grasp for a little improvement, they're missing the bigger picture. So why are we continuing to tinker with and tweak a system that needs to be transformed? For one thing, more work and new responsibilities get added to our academic and administrative load every year. Everyone working in a school is increasingly expected to do more, often with much less. Administrators are devoting large chunks of time not only to improving students' academic performance, supervising their staff, and addressing safety issues but also to addressing increasing numbers of mental health issues. As discussed in the previous chapters, the psychological and behavioral challenges presented by many students require considerable care and attention, much more than was ever expected just a decade ago.

This forward-focused approach can be seen in everything from our agrarian-society school calendar to our daily bell schedule. Sure, it's the way we experienced school. It's the way our students' parents experienced school. But sticking to these norms is preventing us from taking the big, bold leap that's required to successfully deliver our students into the challenges and rigors of the twenty-first century.

We all know that our education system should—actually must—change in order to help our students succeed. Yet we spend year after year in a forward-focused mode. Why haven't we yet flipped the switch to a future-focused outlook? Here are some of the root causes for our inability to take the necessary steps toward the future:

- State and federal legislation keeps us focused on traditional assessments and locks us into traditional cultures, structures, and rules.
- We are holding beliefs—some might even say nostalgia—about what school should be. Teachers and parents who did just fine in a system that met their needs twenty or thirty years ago are disinclined to take risks on something entirely different. "It worked for me" is a phrase that should be banished from school board meetings for now and all time!
- There's unwillingness to exert the considerable effort needed to change what seems like a "good," "pretty good," or at least "good enough" system.
- Within a system that reinforces and rewards compliance and rule following, few people can maintain the will to agitate for a bolder vision of the future.
- Although legislators have seen fit to tinker with many aspects of our current education system, they still haven't found a way to successfully legislate innovation. Therefore, it's up to us to figure out a way to instill innovation in our schools.

These are all surprisingly stubborn issues that have stifled efforts at true school reform and have forced far too many school leaders to be forward focused rather than future focused.

Well-Meaning People, Failed Reform

Rarely a year goes by without another news story about a smart, well-intentioned idealist who sets out to reform education—and fails. There are many reasons why changing our system is such a difficult task, but I often find a common thread among these stories. When you look closer, you'll see that many of these reformers failed to consider the structural and cultural "regularities" of school. They failed to take into account the inherent asymmetrical power relationship between teachers and students that has characterized tax-supported public schools for at least two centuries.

EXPERT IM

For many people, there's a sense that schools worked for them, and it's a system that made our country great. But we can't continue to go on in the way we have been. We need to have the culture of a start-up in our schools. We need to be the agents of change.

—Ray McNulty
Former Vermont commissioner of education and a current senior fellow at ICLE

Daily schedules of forty-two-minute periods; teachers asking questions far more than students during lessons; textbooks, homework, and frequent tests—these features are what Yale professor Seymour Sarason calls the *regularities* of schooling, and they persist generation after generation.[1] It's easy to underestimate the power of our current school structure and culture, but we do so at our peril. Designers of reform seldom think about the inherent stability of the institution they want to transform.

Given a Promotion or Assigned Detention?

To better understand this trap and the limitations with our regularities of school, let me take a moment to point out a simple instance of technology moving faster than education norms. The following is an example of how analog education is failing our digital natives: consider restrictions on students' use of Google to get answers and our mandates against texting to or sharing answers with fellow students. In our current version of school, what do we call this? That's right: cheating.

But is it? Anyone who spends even a day working on a design, production, or leadership team will soon be Googling information and sharing that information with coworkers. These are twenty-first-century success skills—using available resources to find answers and collaborating effectively in a team setting. Why do the skills that can earn us a *promotion* at work lead to children being disciplined at school? The reason is that we haven't yet found a way to educate digital natives in anything other than an outdated, analog way. We need to rethink how we use technology and then how to employ it to prepare kids for the world they'll live in, not the world we used to live in. This is being future focused!

But how do we adopt this new type of focus?

A New Focus: A New Mindset

To embody this type of future focus, we need to start with a new, growth-oriented mindset. The idea of a growth mindset was popularized by Stanford professor Carol Dweck in her best seller, *Mindset: The New Psychology of Success.* I recommend that you read this terrific book to learn more about adopting a growth mindset. But for now, let's look at how your mindset affects your approach to planning and implementing change. As each new challenge or situation arises in your school day, and as you begin to address it, it's worth asking yourself, *Am I being future focused here? Am I operating out of a growth mindset or a fixed and limited one?*

To truly personify a growth mindset, we must envision solutions, strategies, and proposals in terms of long-range time frames that extend beyond the average one- or two-year planning session. We must prepare ourselves to anticipate what future knowledge and skills will be most needed. And we must, at all times, keep that future focus in mind. The following are a few keys to getting this type of change started.

Temet Nosce—Know Thyself

One problem is that all of us who work in schools today were educated in the past. And the great majority of us are products of the American education system. We're people who liked school so much when we were kids that we ended up devoting our careers to working in the same setting. We're people who went on to college to major in "school," and when we graduated, we ended up full circle, hoping to make an impact on students' lives just the way our own teachers had done for us.

As noble as this career circle is, it's also fixed in the past. The following are a few quick questions to ask yourself as a reality check: If you're a teacher, are you instructing much as you were instructed as a student? If you're an administrator, are you doing your job pretty much the same way you saw it being done by principals during your years as a student? If your answer is yes, your perspective and your way of working are very much rooted in the past even though you may feel you want to operate with a future focus.

But don't despair. Being honest about this conflict is half the battle—and perhaps the most important half. I commend your courage if you can admit that your mindset is more "forward" than "future" right now.

You'll know you're ready to change when you realize you want to stop preparing your students for a bygone era. And if you can build enough momentum with your colleagues, superiors, and/or reports, you'll begin dismantling an education system controlled by rules, regulations, certifications, terms, and formal legal agreements. No longer will you be part of an immovable system that's fixed in the past. With this new mindset, you'll be able to look to the future with more of an entrepreneurial mindset and properly prepare for growth.

This entrepreneurial mindset is essential in your approach to district and school organization, decision-making, and action-taking. It will liberate you and your colleagues from the outdated systems and structures that keep you stuck in the past. And when you begin acting like an entrepreneur within your own classroom, school, or district, you begin to mirror the entrepreneurial attitudes and behaviors that your students will need in the future to navigate successful careers and lives.

Put a Stake in It

As you work toward changing from a fixed to a growth mindset—from being forward focused to being future focused—lift your eyes from the track in front of you and allow yourself to gaze into the future. Put a stake in the ground three to five years out, or even as many as eight. Then devise a system focused on what students must know, do, and be like over that period to succeed in this technology-based, information-based, rapidly changing society.

It's important to remember that you can't build something new without being willing to let go of the old. The mission of a future-focused approach is to clear away whatever is obstructing your ability to bring to life a vision that makes education meaningful and worthwhile for your students.

Inspire Lifelong Learning

I know I touched on the evolution of jobs and careers in chapter 2, but take a quick look at this list of ten jobs that are popular right now with young professionals:

- Social media manager
- Podcaster
- App designer
- Artificial intelligence/chatbot copywriter
- Influencer
- CGI illustrator
- SEO content writer
- YouTube personality
- Drone photographer
- E-commerce designer

Notice anything about these jobs?

Yes, they're all, in some form or another, tech based. But the answer I was looking for is that not a single one of these jobs existed twenty years ago.

This means that when many of the young people who currently hold these jobs were in kindergarten, none of their teachers could begin to prepare them for these roles. Why? They didn't yet exist. It's worth asking ourselves what new jobs will exist in twenty years. But the reality is that we don't know. So instead of preparing kids for a defined job—or set of jobs—we need to be preparing kids for an uncertain career arc. We need to give them the skills necessary to be agile thinkers and skilled collaborators. Consequently, we need to help them become lifelong learners, able to adjust and prosper as job demands change.

EXPERT IM

We in education are hesitant to rethink school, even when it comes to basic things we already know we can improve. We know that not every subject needs the same amount of time to learn. It's now possible to build master schedules using technology that allow all kids to have different-length periods throughout the day. But schools are hesitant to adopt these innovations.

—David Bain
Vice president of academic planning & analytics, Houghton Mifflin Harcourt

The stakes are very real. To paraphrase Hall of Fame coach John Wooden, *failing to prepare our students* for an uncertain future is the same as *preparing them to fail* in an uncertain future. We must focus on teaching our students to learn, not on rewarding them for complying with outdated systems that no longer serve their needs. If we can keep that spark alive and create a new generation of lifelong learners, we'll be fostering a generation that will thrive in the workplace, no matter what they do for a living.

The Biggest Roadblock—the Budget

Again and again, I see the same intractable roadblock on the path to making schools work in the twenty-first century: the budget.

More accurately, the roadblock is the mindset *behind* the budget, the one that holds to the belief that the budget is more or less fixed every year. Budgeting based on the previous year stifles innovation and real change, both financially and psychologically. In most districts and schools, as we plan the budget for the next year, we start with last year's budget. We look at our present classrooms, teachers, and instructional programs, and this becomes our point of departure. Then we ask what it will cost to keep the budget in place. Typically, it costs about 2 or 3 percent more each year. We expect a hike of a percentage point or two for general inflation, and another percentage point or two for contracts.

Where will we find the money to fund these cost increases?

We can't cut contract expenses, so we have to look to so-called non-essential expenses. Unfortunately, this often means we chip away at supposedly "less critical" expenditures, such as professional development and related travel, even though these are in fact "critical" factors in achieving academic excellence.

There. Budget done. Now let's put the same plan as last year in place—*and get the same results as last year.* The sad fact is, if we think the budget must stay more or less intact from year to year, we'll never find the resources for real innovation, improvement, and growth.

A Future Based on the Past

When we start with last year's budget (which is really the budget for the year before that, and the year before that, and the year before that, and on and on), we're psychologically and financially prevented from being innovation minded and future focused. Instead, we're budgeting from a fixed mindset that just looks for small, incremental improvements over what we did last year. This is the very definition of building our future based on our past. And here's the heart of the problem: we enter into our annual budgeting exercise with the mindset that the best way to budget is to work with what's already in place. We're conditioned to believe budgets are more or less set in stone. So we focus on moving around the line items, making little tweaks, and doing our best to stretch dollars. If only we could approach this exercise with an understanding of its potential to be a valuable resource that enables and funds innovation and growth, right? Sounds good, but difficult.

Here's how you can do it.

Zero-Based Budgeting: The Ultimate Growth-Mindset Budget

By definition, the zero-based budgeting approach to financial planning liberates your organization from its past and from the annual "tinker and shuffle" ritual that has come to characterize annual budgeting in most schools and districts. And it does this consistently, year after year. Each year brings a reset—an opportunity to create new goals and a fresh budget, then to plan ahead from there. (Remember that stake you put in three, five, or eight years out.) Investopedia defines zero-based budgeting as

> A method of budgeting in which all expenses must be justified for each new period. Zero-based budgeting starts from a "zero base," and every function within an organization is analyzed for its needs and costs. Budgets are then built around what is needed for the upcoming period, regardless of whether the budget is higher or lower than the previous one.[2]

For some time, the most future-focused and leading-edge businesses in the private sector have used zero-based budgeting as a vehicle for efficiency and innovation. Now imagine if you and your colleagues operated in the same way. What if you had to defend each expense, each year? How many of them would you truly want to fight for? How many would you happily toss aside? Zero-based budgeting builds logic and a future focus into the planning process. It ensures that all expenses are relevant and that all are investments in the future, not mere legacy costs or investments in the past. This thinking drives efficiency, as it forces organizations to cut expenses that no longer serve their *current* goals or the future needs of students.

Yet the real power of zero-based budgeting lies in its being built on a foundation of attention to big goals and meaningful changes. This includes consideration of the innovative steps, systems, structures, and staffing necessary to achieve these goals and changes. The process itself encourages continual goal- and innovation-oriented thinking. Just imagine if instead of beginning to build your budget by asking, "What will it cost to keep last year's budget in place?" you instead asked, "What do we need to do and change *right now* to prepare every student in our school for successful careers and lives?"

In terms of the Rigor/Relevance Framework detailed in chapter 4, beginning with last year's budget will all but guarantee that next year's plans won't move beyond Quad A and Quad C, beyond basic understanding and knowledge for its own sake. We're regulated, certified, tenured, and contracted around Quads A and C, so we direct all our financial resources to those priorities and repeatedly find we have no room left to fund Quads B and D, application and adaptation.

This approach may have worked adequately back when preparing students for college was little different from preparing them for careers—when the memorization of facts and the adoption of a few simple skills were enough to excel both in school and in jobs. This may even have worked when we funneled students into large, siloed corporations where specialized knowledge was the key to success. But, as should be clear, the world is very different now than it was in the past. Today, our students need innovative programs and instructional methodologies that focus on Quad B and Quad D skills to thrive in our Quad B and Quad D world.

At this point, I think most of you are on board with this message. But if for some reason you still don't believe me, consider this disturbing story.

My Musty, Dusty Textbook

To prove that a fixed-mindset approach to budgeting and planning traps educators in Quads A and C, I'll share an unsettling story. Back in 1985, when I was a director in the New York Education Department, I coauthored a textbook, *Technology for Tomorrow*, published by South-Western Publishing.

To this day, I still receive royalties from sales of this book. Remarkably, this means that somewhere in this country, teachers and school districts are ordering *Technology for Tomorrow* and are using it in their classrooms. This is despite the fact that the book was written more than a decade before Google was formed and more than two decades before the iPhone was launched.

I'd like to think that the words I wrote were timeless. But I know better. Flipping through the pages of the book today is like reading an ancient stone tablet. That my textbook is still being used in a modern classroom setting is shocking. Why some districts believe that the content from the first half of the 1980s is still relevant is incomprehensible to me, and downright unfair to students. But it's just one example of how educators budget and plan on autopilot, without a thorough analysis of the tools and systems most needed to prepare their students for the future.

How to Implement Change—Realistically

At this point, you may be thinking, *How could it be possible to adopt an entirely new approach to budgeting?* And you're right to consider this question. We're all dismayed at how futile it can be to try to change something as mundane as the current bell schedule in our building. How could we expect to ever overhaul the budgeting process?

The answer is, we can't—at least not all at once and not straight away. I understand that budgets and educational programming are hemmed in by contracts, policies, and laws. I understand that credentialing requirements put real limits on who can teach what, when, where, and how. But there are ways to move forward. I encourage you to experiment where you can in making change, in evolving the process. And that's one key: evolutionary change tends to be more comfortable and less threatening to most people, and therefore more likely to succeed. Experiment where there's room and with those who have an appetite for it. Be patient, but deliberate. Be bold, but intentional. Take baby steps and calculated risks. But just be sure to start *somewhere.* The following sections offer a few ideas for making this start.

A Lesson from the Most Innovative Schools

This attitude of just starting somewhere is a hallmark of the nation's most rapidly improving schools. Highly innovative schools I've been privileged to work with through the years have figured out how and where they can break the rules. They acknowledge when the old system isn't working, and they start experimenting with new systems or strategies. But they don't do it overnight, and they don't change everything at once. What sets these schools apart is that they start with the manageable goal of getting unstuck. To break free of inertia, you need to take a step—any step, no matter how small. This means taking some sort of action with the accepted knowledge that things must change in order for your school or district to improve.

EXPERT IM

One of our findings was that teachers don't feel empowered to be creative in their teaching techniques. But the more teachers feel empowered to be creative in their application of technology, it trickles down to student engagement. The magic comes when you roll out a plan for the future and get teachers familiar and comfortable with how they can innovate in the classroom.

—Tom Matson
Senior executive leadership strategist, Gallup Education

How can you get started? Sit down with key members of your team and commit to asking again and again where there is some wiggle room for experimentation. Don't give up until you've pinpointed at least a few areas in the budget where you can toss out the old norms and squeeze in some new goals, then budget and tweak systems and structures to achieve these goals.

From there, I suggest starting with the top one-third of educators who have the desire and disposition for rolling up their sleeves, tackling new challenges, and implementing real changes—all while assuming leadership along the way. You know this one-third by their enthusiasm for exploring new solutions or trying out new concepts. They're the creative ones, the fearless ones—and the ones who can be the "bell cows" for leading others along the path toward change.

What typically happens is that once this top third has smoothly transitioned into a new and effective way of doing things, the middle third, the cautious "wait-and-see" crowd, will warm to the changes and join in. Make no mistake: this wait-and-see crowd is important. They're the ones who want to take things slow and steady, and overthink any new idea. This means that many of your more cautious staff will listen to them. But at heart, this group is curious and willing to try out new ideas once they've been proven to be viable.

Then there's the final third—the stubborn ones. They're the ones who will dig in their heels. They have their ways of doing things, so they prefer that you take your change elsewhere, thank you very much. That said, most will give in to change if they find themselves in the conspicuous minority of naysayers. Or they'll move on. Mindful implementation and subtle pressure are usually the winning strategies for this crew.

Lone Star Innovation

For a great source of inspiration in chipping away at the old system and replacing it with one designed around innovation, consider the Districts of Innovation concept in Texas. Created in 2015, this program makes selected districts eligible for exemption from a number of state statutes. Within some defined limits, participating schools are free to make decisions that catalyze greater efficiency and help them better serve their students. What this means in practical terms is that districts

- Gain greater control in determining the educational and instructional models appropriate for their students.
- Enjoy certain freedoms and increased flexibility, still with accountability, relative to state mandates that dictate educational programming.
- Receive the tremendous gift of thinking and acting creatively, openly, differently, and outside the rigidity of certain standards, contracts, and credentials.

This is an important mandate that gives schools powerful new tools. Here's an example I love from one of the Districts of Innovation schools: Jason Massey teaches automotive technology at Dripping Springs High School. Massey has worked in the automotive field for fifteen years. He even owns his own business designing and building race cars. His students are, in my opinion, very lucky. From Massey, they receive an interdisciplinary, relevant, and current view of automotive technologies, one that includes business skills, customer insights, and real-world market and industry challenges and opportunities. Massey knows from experience how technologies are changing what people need to be successful in the automotive industry, both today *and* tomorrow.

Here's the interesting part: Massey lacks the state teaching certificate usually required to teach a specific subject in Texas. But thanks to Districts of Innovation and the bold leaders behind the decision to hire him, students spend time with a teacher who is supremely qualified to instruct an automotive technology class. Thanks to the loosening of restrictions in the name of innovation, Massey is free to share his practical knowledge and know-how with students.

For additional information on being future focused rather than forward focused, you can download a Successful Practices Network and American Association of School Administrators case study of Maine Township High School District at the following website: https://www.aasa.org/uploadedFiles/Resources/Successful_Practices_Network/AASA-Case-Study-Maine-Township.pdf.

Use ESSA to Your Advantage

Not every state has a program like the Districts of Innovation initiative. But, no matter where you live, there are always opportunities to implement a more entrepreneurial mindset. With your future focus firmly in place, you don't need to worry about what's *not* available. Instead, ask yourself—and your colleagues—how you can get started with what you *already have.*

For example, we all have the federal Every Student Succeeds Act (ESSA). Although not without its faults, ESSA is a landmark in one key way: it gives more control back to states and local districts to determine how educators will monitor and evaluate student learning and progress. ESSA has blown the door wide open for candid conversations with local school boards, colleagues, and communities to create new ways of achieving and measuring performance improvement for students, schools, and districts.

Of course, ESSA doesn't give you carte blanche to overhaul your school or district in any and every way you see fit. But remember what the most successful entrepreneurs do—they seize see an opportunity where others see a barrier. Consider ESSA an opening to begin experimenting with that top one-third of teachers who are willing to try new strategies or solutions. Keep in mind what the nation's most rapidly improving schools do—they begin *somewhere.*

Anyone who works with young people understands that students are the hope of the future—theirs, ours, and our nation's. Therefore, we need to be future focused in our planning and execution. We must nurture students. We must inspire them to continually learn, and provide them with the capacity to take action with their knowledge. We must steer them toward recognizing the open doors of opportunity, while they learn how to open new doors of their own. We can't do this by continuing to use a twentieth-century model of education and making incremental changes to twentieth-century strategies. We need to be bold. We need to act on the future. And the heartening truth is, being bold requires only one initial step—no matter how small—toward a new way of thinking.

LESSONS FOR THE FUTURE

- Whereas the majority of education systems focus their energy on making incremental improvements to the way things have always been done (forward focus), what is required of us now is to transform our systems in bold new ways that look toward the needs of our twenty-first-century student body (future focus).
- We need to rethink how we use technology and then employ it to prepare kids for the world they'll live in, not the world we've come from. If we're using Google every day on the job, why are students prohibited from using it? If we huddle up with teammates to solve a problem at work, why are students punished for collaborating on a test? What we call cheating is now often a success skill.

- School budgets need to move from the annual tinker-and-shuffle approach to one of zero-based budgeting, in which all expenses must be justified for each new budgeting period.
- Get started with what you have, and look to innovative districts, such as Texas Districts of Innovation, to inspire you for the future. To help you do this, consider joining the AASA National Innovation Network.
- Take at least one step, no matter how small, to get unstuck. Moving toward a growth mindset and becoming future focused is about steady progress, not making a ground-breaking leap.

6

Growth over Proficiency

Take a look around the natural world, and you'll quickly come to the conclusion that variety is the name of the game. Animals can be as tall as a giraffe or as low to the ground as a rattlesnake. Trees can grow as big as a redwood or as diminutive as a dwarf willow. We accept the idea that in nature, each thing grows the way it needs to, when it needs to. Then why won't we extend that idea to our students? We'd laugh at a farmer for expecting a radish crop to grow as tall as a corn crop, and at exactly the same pace. Yet we consistently treat students with a "one size fits all" approach, expecting the same progressive development and level of proficiency from each member of a class.

Imagine for a moment that it's the first day of sixth grade at a school near you. At the start of the day, thirty young people file into a classroom. Sixty eyes train themselves on the teacher at the front of the room. The work of the school year is about to begin. What can we expect to have happen?

Anyone who has taught in a classroom understands that each child arrives in that room with a unique set of abilities and capacities, a unique amount of energy and focus. Each lives in a different home, with a uniquely different life within that home. They bring along all the knowledge and skills gained during previous school years, as well as all the ways they've been helped or hindered by every educational situation they've encountered. The previous grade left each of these students in a different place. Some excelled. Some gave up. Most were encouraged and directed to improve, not just academically but also socially and emotionally.

The students in that classroom on the first day of school will each have a different experience throughout the upcoming school year. Some have parents who support them in every possible way, ensuring that they receive what they need to thrive. Some have parents whose overinvolvement will set off feelings of anxiety and powerlessness. Some live in homes where economic stress has reached the breaking point. Some are in abusive situations that are taking an increasing toll on their mental and physical health. Some may be experiencing homelessness and living in shelters.

Students run the gamut, so why are standards all the same? It's widely understood, among academics and nonacademics alike, that we learn in different ways and at different speeds. Yet many in education insist on following a proficiency model that anticipates grade completion, with little variation allowed. No matter how effective the classroom teacher may be, there always will be disparities in the knowledge, attitudes, and skills that students draw upon to meet grade-specific goals.

Measurement, of course, is one of the most effective forms of assessment. But it's my belief that our educational assessments often are measuring the wrong things. We all understand that true learning is not just a case of "facts in, knowledge out." Each set of neurological, physiological, and emotional markers contributes uniquely to the overall development of a student. In a classroom filled with more than two dozen five-, ten-, or fifteen-year-olds, some students will grasp concepts immediately and begin to apply them right away. Others will grasp that same knowledge more slowly, until they finally have a holistic understanding of the material and feel comfortable applying it. Yet other students will slip further and further behind, as the classroom races to meet the next set of standards. This is something we already know. All students learn in different ways, at different paces, and from different cues. Yet we continue to rank and measure students using one-size-fits-all grade-level standards. Why? I believe many of us as educators have blurred the distinction between the concept of growth and that of proficiency, causing us to lose sight of our true purpose in educating children.

Our Purpose Is Growth

For two such seemingly simple terms, there's a surprising amount of controversy around *proficiency* and *growth*. On the surface, the distinction seems straightforward: proficiency assesses whether or not a stated goal has been achieved. There's the same goal for everyone, and a student either meets the standard or doesn't. Growth, by contrast, looks at the trend of achievement over time, measuring the progress of an individual or group.

Many educators are pushing back against the idea of measuring achievement through a one-size-fits-all standard that's established by the Department of Education. They feel that this proficiency model inevitably punishes struggling schools and at-risk students. Uniform standards, applied across the board, can fail to recognize the context provided by historical, economic, regional, or socioeconomic factors. Even if performance is improving and there is growth in key sectors, a student who misses the mark on a unilateral standard is considered to be noncompliant, even if he or she is making real progress.

Take, for example, a fourth-grade student who begins the year reading at the first-grade level. This student is fortunate enough to have a fantastic teacher who does an amazing job, and by the end of the year, he is reading at the third-grade level. This is tremendous growth. But now we sit this student down to take a proficiency test that measures whether he can read at an end-of-fourth-grade level. Of course, the student can't. Now the school, class, teacher, and student look and feel like failures, and no credit is given for the child advancing two years in a single year.

By contrast, assessing for growth as the method to evaluate students, schools, and districts allows a "personal best" model to emerge, one in which each assessment is based on progress toward improvement, not toward a universal standard. That's why I'm a proponent of focusing on growth, as it's an inherently more meaningful measure for all students at every level.

This idea of growth and individual progress sounds great, but I don't want to minimize the realities of the classroom. I'm certainly aware that in our current climate, many classroom teachers are being directed to teach to the standards, no matter what the next most appropriate lesson for an individual's growth might be. Yes, standards are uniform. Standards are easy to measure. But standards should not be the focus. Growth should be.

Right now, a typical sixth-grade classroom might have three kids ready to learn eighth-grade standards, a few ready for seventh-grade standards, ten ready for sixth-grade standards, and a few who are still struggling even to meet fourth-grade standards. Given what we have to anticipate will always be a wide range of classroom diversity, and given the rigidity of the standards required to be taught, what can administrators and teachers do?

When something isn't working—and I think we can all agree that our current proficiency model is not working—it can be helpful to take a step back and ask ourselves, *What is the purpose of what we are doing?* When I ask third-grade teachers, they tell me that their purpose is to prepare their students for fourth grade. When I ask fourth-grade teachers, they tell me it's to get students ready for fifth grade. It goes on like this right up to the high school teachers who tell me that the purpose of teaching upper grade levels in high school is to provide students with all the preparation they'll need to go to college or get a job.

But this is not where our focus should be—to just get them to the next level. We all know that no matter what our role in the education system, no matter the age of the students we work with, our true purpose is to prepare them for successful careers and lives. I also believe that we have been living for so long under the blanket of credentials and contracts that we've been forced to take our eyes off this purpose. We're distracted by standardized tests, evaluations, and contract requirements. Before we know it, we're so focused on these other demands that we've lost sight of the long-term goals, dreams, and hopes we have for our students.

The root of the problem is this: the system is arranged to keep the purpose of school and instruction focused on little more than advancing students grade by grade toward graduation. We're credentialed and contracted to keep solely focused on getting students to achieve the milestones that will allow them to enter the next grade. We do this even though we understand in our hearts that it's impossible to apply a single metric or universal standard to something as intricate and multifaceted as human development. Yet our schools measure, rank, and sort students into finite categories more than ever before.

The result? School has become an end in itself, not a means to an end. The purpose of school has become school itself—and this is a big mistake.

Multidimensional Learners

Remember that farmer I mentioned at the beginning of the chapter, the one with the field of radishes and the field of corn? He knows that each field requires different methods to encourage growth—using a particular type of soil, scheduling the correct frequency of watering, determining fertilizer proportions, and more. At the end of a season, he'll be pleased if each radish has burrowed into the ground and produced a fat, crispy root vegetable. And he'll marvel when the corn is truly as high as an elephant's eye. He won't be angry at the radish for not growing in tall stalks. And he won't be frustrated at the corn for the way it needs constant fertilization to thrive. Each plant grew the way it needed to, helped along by a committed professional who understood how to create the ideal conditions that allowed it to thrive.

We can do the same in our classrooms too, as soon as we abandon the rigid adherence to proficiency and instead look to a model of growth. We all saw the limitations of the standards-based proficiency model with the latest scores from the National Assessment of Education Progress (NAEP).[1] Educators and policymakers within the standards movement were stunned that scores dropped even though we've continued to place ever-higher value on standards and proficiency-based instruction and to put more effort into this model. Clearly, the proficiency-based learning model is too restrictive. It ignores the reality that children are wonderfully varied in how they develop and how they learn.

An education system that treats every student as a cog in an automated machine is in danger of forgetting that students are unique and valuable individuals. We're often operating as if education were just one more type of factory, spitting out graduated students like widgets. There's evidence of this mindset in our continued drive toward even greater standardization and measurement. Standardization smooths everything and everyone into a bland average that's devoid of the spikes and curves that actually characterize the amazing variety of talents we've been given.

EXPERT IM

We have standard-aligned school systems, but we certainly don't have standard-aligned students. Our learning models have become too narrow. We say, "If you're age twelve, these are the lessons you must receive." But that approach ignores what we know about the developmental nature of learning.

—David Bain
Vice president of academic planning & analytics, Houghton Mifflin Harcourt

Todd Rose is the cofounder and president of the Center for Individual Opportunity and a faculty member at the Harvard Graduate School of Education. In his book *The End of Average: How We Succeed in a World That Values Sameness*, he observes:

> Just about any meaningful human characteristic—especially talent—consists of multiple dimensions. The problem is that when trying to measure talent, we frequently resort to the average, reducing our jagged talent profile to a single dimension like the score on a standardized test or grades or a job performance ranking. But when we succumb to this kind of one-dimensional thinking, we end up in deep trouble.[2]

All too often, our schools have reinforced our natural predilection for this type of "one-dimensional thinking" by encouraging us to compare children's merit on simple scales—grades, standardized tests, and the like. Later in his book, Rose adds, ". . . if our goal is to nurture individual excellence, then weak correlations tell us something different: we will only succeed if we pay attention to the distinct jaggedness of every individual."[3]

I see the truth of this "distinct jaggedness" concept in my own personal experience. My children and grandchildren run the gamut from intellectually gifted and talented to severely disabled, and everything in between. Each of them absorbs and applies knowledge at a unique pace. That's because their learning style is part of a cumulative process that's part and parcel with who they are. Some of them start applying knowledge as soon as they're exposed to initial foundational steps. Others can apply knowledge only when the final pieces of the puzzle click into place. One learning style or speed isn't necessarily better than the other; they're just different. And the outcome needs to be the same for all children: to learn, grow, and prosper.

I'm sure you've observed a similar range within your own family. Those of you who are parents of more than one child are in an excellent position to understand my point here. Even having the same biological parents, the same home environment, and the same upbringing, your kids will excel and need help in different areas. And, as a good parent, you don't demand that each one of them pursue the same interests or achieve the same milestones in the same way. One family of six kids could produce a medical doctor, a stay-at-home parent, an artist, an accountant, a comedian, and a ski instructor. Same inputs, vastly different outputs. This should be expected. More, it should be encouraged.

A Lifetime of Learning

I've touched on this in previous chapters, but it's critical for all of us to understand that in the future, the best job candidates will be the ones who understand how to learn and grow—and how to keep on growing throughout their lifetimes. Learning software company Instructure surveyed 750 US-based managers to investigate what they look for when evaluating millennial job candidates. As reported by Instructure vice president Jeff Weber:

> When we asked managers what factors are most important to career success—not simply what they look for in hiring—managers ranked industry knowledge and technical skill on par with core attributes. This suggests that in order to succeed at work, employers want millennials who can demonstrate a well-rounded capacity and interest in continual learning, because the skills they need to do their job now may be vastly different than the ones they need in five to ten years.[4]

In chapter 2, we examined the skills students will need to succeed in the future, such as critical thinking skills, an ability to collaborate, and a deep understanding of evolving technology. But in a much broader sense, the true skill set of the twenty-first century will the ability to learn across careers, across technologies, and throughout life. As I've mentioned before, we don't even know what most jobs of the future will look like. Every student who hopes to be successful in this environment will need a nimble learning style. As MaryEllen Elia, former commissioner of education of the state of New York, said, "We need to produce students who can be successful in the environments they're going to live in, which are very different than those their own teachers grew up in and are living in now."

Employers need employees who can grow. In the future, companies will have access to all the ubiquitous automation and artificial intelligence they require. What they'll need from their staff is the ability to stay ahead of the curve with flexible learning styles, not adherence to standards that are outdated almost as soon as they're created.

Given this dynamic work climate, we have to adjust our methods to prepare students for successful careers and lives, not just prepare them to take the next test and move on to the next grade. Our focus therefore must be on growth. The importance of this change becomes even clearer when we consider the difference between instruction and learning. Planning only to the point of instruction ensures that teachers *instruct,* but it doesn't account for how our instruction will be received. By contrast, planning to the point of learning is designed to focus on whether or not students actually *learn.* When we think of instruction as ultimately being about learning, then students remain at the center of our academic planning and decision-making. This may seem like a small distinction, but instruction puts the focus on us doing the instructing. Learning, by contrast, reminds us that education is about the students, not us.

In the most successful classrooms in America, this process is already under way, thanks to teachers who understand the true nature of their work. As Ray McNulty, former Vermont commissioner of education, current president of the Successful Practices Network, and a senior fellow at ICLE, has observed, "Lifelong learners are built through self-directed learning, which happens when teachers realize that they need to move from pedagogy, which is learning controlled by the teacher, to learning that's controlled by the students." These types of self-directed learners then become adult learners.

By keeping the focus on learning—on growth—we're more likely to make lifelong learners of the students we teach. And that's the key for them to be career ready in the twenty-first century. As the Instructure survey showed, employers recognize that the skills employees need will change and evolve throughout the course of their employment. What matters more than proficiency in test taking is the desire and ability to learn—and to learn again and again over the course of a career.

Measuring for Growth

Helping students achieve growth rather than mere proficiency begins by finding ways to encourage them to grow within the framework of their own unique situation. This includes ways to track and assess growth, as well as cultivate it. The idea of a growth mindset, as developed by Stanford professor Carol Dweck, was outlined in the previous chapter. And when thinking about growth—what it means and its many benefits—this is a great model. But it speaks more to a personal approach to achievement, rather than to a systemic approach to focusing on growth in the larger context of a classroom, school, or district.

In the classrooms I've been using as examples throughout this chapter, growth might mean very different things for each one of the students. For some, it might be finally mastering double-digit multiplication. For others, it might be finally grasping basic principles of addition that were confusing to them in earlier grades. And for yet another group, it might mean exploring an introduction to algebra—and learning to love it. Now extrapolate that out to multiple classrooms, possibly in multiple schools. With this disparate group, how can you as a school leader help foster growth throughout a system that's been tied to proficiency?

One way is to rethink what you measure.

Before we dive into measuring growth, let me make one thing clear: measuring growth will never be as easy as measuring proficiency. As you probably understand at this point, proficiency is a very limited snapshot with clear parameters, often with both a "ceiling" and a "floor." You pass, or you don't pass. You meet the requirements, or you don't meet them. You fall within this acceptable scale, or you don't. This is easy to track, compare, and judge.

This ease of measurement is why we've seen many districts implement core standards or grade-level standards along with assessments that were designed to measure those standards. The problem, of course, is that many students aren't at a point in their development where the standards are appropriate. It's possible to have whole schools—or districts—that have already moved beyond the standards (above the ceiling). At the same time, many schools or districts may be years behind the standards (below the floor). These disparities have caused 80 percent of school districts to purchase supplementary assessment systems to help them determine what they're missing with the grade-level standards.

EXPERT IM

We have a research team that thinks about how existing and emerging technologies impact what needs to be learned and how people learn. The growth trajectory is incredibly important. We need methods for measuring growth on basic things like reading and math, and also for social and developmental areas.

—Karen Cator
President and CEO, Digital Promise.

The good news is we've made real advances in our ability to pinpoint and track growth over time. One example of progress being made in this area comes from MetaMetrics, creator of the Lexile Framework for Reading (https://lexile.com).

It's a research-driven, scientific system for reading and listening that helps educators and parents match students with books, articles, and other leveled reading resources. Readers and materials are assigned a score on the Lexile scale, in which lower scores reflect easier readability for books and lower reading ability for readers. Why does this matter? Because noting the Lexile measure of a text can assist teachers in selecting targeted materials that present an appropriate level of challenge for a reader—not so difficult as to be frustrating, yet difficult enough to challenge the reader and encourage real, measurable growth.

More important, we can use systems like the Lexile Framework to track growth. If we know a child's Lexile score in seventh grade, we can use a data analytics system to predict where that child will be at high school graduation. How? The seventh-grade score may be a quantitative snapshot from a moment in one individual student's learning timeline, but when a database contains three million scores, as the Lexile system does, from other students who were at the same point in their learning timelines, it can predict an individual student's growth trajectory into the future.

Going a step further, as we add more data points to the system, we can begin to see which learning interventions can accelerate our seventh-grade student's trajectory, and apply these interventions to other students on a similar pathway. Because of this predictive capability, the Lexile Framework can be used to project student growth through middle school, high school, and college—all the way up to entering the workforce. For an example of what this type of projection looks like, see figures 6.1 and 6.2. (As an aside, it's interesting to note that, as these two figures show, the reading requirements for entry-level jobs are now actually higher than those for first-year college courses—a fact few people are aware of.)

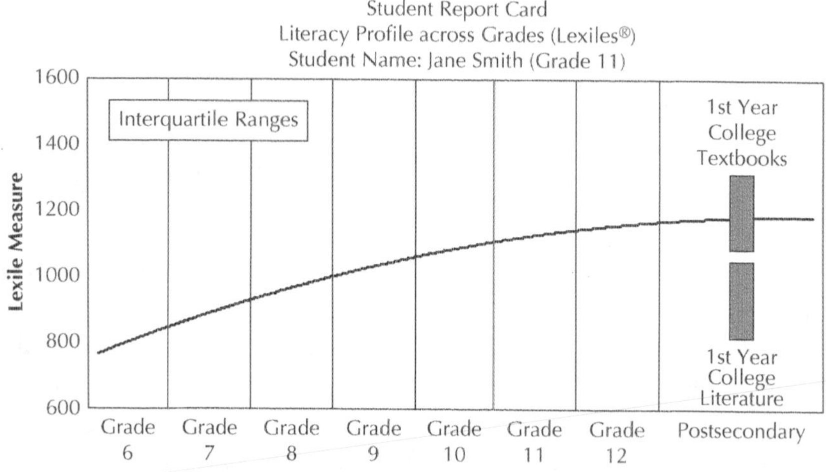

FIGURE 6.1 Literacy—College Readiness

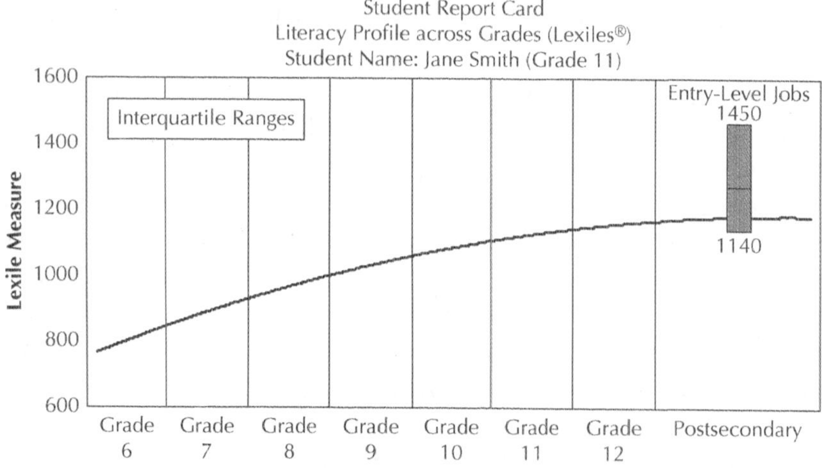

FIGURE 6.2 Literacy—Career Readiness

Think of the Lexile Framework as being similar to the ability of Google Maps to tell you the best route to take from your home to the baseball park or the movie theater. Google's recommendation is made based on your current position and on the experience of thousands—or hundreds of thousands—of people who previously made the same journey. I'll provide more on the predictive power of data in the next chapter. For now, the main point is that we're beginning to develop the data-based tools needed to track, assess, and promote growth in schools. These are powerful new technologies, but they still need to be augmented by more humanistic approaches to cultivating growth in students.

Make It (More) Fun

When students experience success, at whatever level, they're typically happier in school. And when they like school, they stay in school. This makes perfect sense to most of us, but you have to admit that the system hasn't been set up to promote anything even remotely resembling a love of learning. In fact, we often promote just the opposite, with students who too often feel antipathy toward the education system long after graduation. But there are small changes we can make right away to turn things around. And when we do, we take a big step toward promoting growth in students.

Success Leads to Growth

Samuel Houston, the president and CEO of the North Carolina Science, Mathematics, and Technology Education Center, told me about a time he was asked to lead a school in which the faculty seemed almost to take pride in withholding passing grades. "I told them," he said, "we've got to find a way to make every kid in this school feel successful." He asked the teachers to find a way to give a pop quiz every day that they knew the students would pass. The reason was simple. "If they can be a part of a successful learning environment and be proud of their work or a problem they solved, they'll become more successful." The faculty was skeptical at first. But it worked. They created successful learners who were positioned to become even more successful because they believed in themselves and their capabilities.

EXPERT IM

The simple fact is that if we're going to be successful with supporting kids in their overall development and growth, they need to like school. Bam! That's it. They need to like it. School needs to be fun.

—Shauna McDonald
Executive director, Playworks Minnesota

If your goal is to focus on growth for your students, think of ways that you can help them feel successful as learners. This not only gives them a sense of pride but also helps them self-identify as learners. Once they begin to see themselves as successful learners, their sense of agency increases, often making them more self-directed.

Ready for Life, Not Better at School

Take a moment to think of what happens when a student is struggling academically in a core curriculum subject (e.g., math, science, or language arts). The first thing we do is pull her out of her elective classes, which are usually the courses she likes, and make her double up on the subjects in which she's experiencing failure. We remove her from music, where she plays an instrument in the band and learns about collaboration and creativity. We remove her from sports, where she works with her team to reach a collective goal. We tell her she can't take any more art classes until she pulls up her grades, even though the art studio is the one place in the entire school building where she feels that she has a home. And we put her back to working in isolation on a subject she hates.

What does this approach do to students? It makes them dislike school even more. It also makes subjects like math and science feel like punishment, not fascinating fields that encourage excitement and discovery. We do this because we're trying to get them to be better at school, not ready for life. There is a more effective way. I have a grandson who loves basketball—so much so, he's convinced that one day he'll play in the NBA, even though he'll only be about 5'7" tall fully grown! At school, though, he was struggling with math and science. How did educators at his school respond?

They gave him two periods of basketball.

Yes, you read that right: two periods of basketball. But one period was coached by a math teacher, and the other was coached by a science teacher. In the end, basketball is a game of numbers, of geometry and physics. Can you guess what happened? He started to look forward to math and science class! By giving the subjects relevance and putting him in a position to succeed, his teachers turned what could have been a punitive experience into an opportunity for growth and self-directed learning.

The Right Feedback, the Right Response

One important key to fostering growth is to be deliberate in how teachers offer feedback. According to John Hattie, whose work I cited in chapter 4, we need to change the mindset that every student should experience at least a year's worth of growth for a year's worth of input. In addition, he says, we need to rethink our attitude toward feedback. Instead of getting out our red pens and having a field day showing students what they've done wrong, we can reframe the situation by communicating the philosophy that errors and mistakes are nothing more than opportunities for learning.

"The major point many of us miss—and I missed it too for a long time—is that in feedback, we need to understand how the receiver is understanding and using the feedback," he told me. "So much is given, yet so little is received." Hattie and his team in New Zealand developed an elementary and high school assessment with three areas of focus: informing teachers of growth and achievement, triangulation with other measures or with other teachers' interpretations, and comparisons with like students over time and levels of achievement.

Hattie's model distinguishes among these three feedback questions:

1. *Where am I going?* (What does success look like?)
2. *How am I going?* (What are the diagnostics relative to where I need to be?)
3. *Where am I going next?* (How can I bridge this gap?)

In Hattie's model, the third element (*Where next?*) builds on the previous two. He believes that students will achieve success when feedback is aligned with the instructional cycle—whether during the task, in process, or during self-regulation. And, interestingly, he notes that mixing praise with feedback possibly has a negative impact. This is because students recall the praise, but are likely to pass over the helpful information on how to improve their performance. Instead, he suggests providing praise separately from constructive feedback.

Choose Growth

It's clear to many of us in this field that when we focus on proficiency, we're no longer measuring students' critical thinking skills or true engagement with the material. Worse, we're depriving teachers of their agency and robbing education of its humanity. When we insist that teachers address only content that can be measured with standardized tests, while we avoid more analytical material, we're hindering the possibility of a deeper, richer life of learning. And, in no small measure, we're devaluing the profession of teaching. We're transforming it into nothing more than test preparation.

As we all know, the reality is that students are individuals with unique gifts, interests, and potential, whether they're struggling with the absolute basics or testing off the charts in terms of achievement. They are, each and every one of them, capable of lasting, authentic growth. They're all capable of making a contribution to society and to their community. If we accept a system that chooses "winners"—students who have cracked the proficiency code of standardized tests and high GPAs—then we're sure to create a disheartened generation of young people, many of whom feel slow, marginalized, or left behind.

Schools and school leaders who choose growth over proficiency, regardless of the challenges, have an opportunity to prepare students to be independent and successful adults in the face of an ever-changing career landscape—our ultimate purpose in education. These will be the schools that dare to dream big, discuss the impractical, innovate solutions, and begin to craft workable plans for the success of all students. The only way to know whether we're reaching this goal, of course, is by effectively measuring ourselves along the way. In the next chapter, we'll address the topic of data and metrics.

LESSONS FOR THE FUTURE

- Students run the gamut in terms of learning speed and style, yet we rely on a proficiency-based system that expects everyone to test at the same level on the same day.
- Instead of focusing on proficiency and meeting standards, we must pay attention to student growth.
- Right now, we're instructing with the purpose of moving students to the next grade level, instead of encouraging the development of a foundation for lifelong learning.

- Measuring growth is more difficult than measuring proficiency. But there are already some leaders in the use of growth-based data and data analytics, such as the MetaMetrics Lexile Framework for Reading. These systems match students with appropriate materials and predict a student's developmental trajectory.
- For us to successfully support learning and growth, kids need to like school. It's as simple as that. This means that we as educators need to try to make students feel successful; avoid addressing core weaknesses with punishment; and offer clear, constructive feedback.

7

Data: The Driver of School and District Decisions

Among the many changes the global coronavirus pandemic brought to everyone's attention was an increased understanding of the importance of data. Newspaper headlines and television reporters spouted such phrases as "doubling rate" and "flattening the curve. " Graphs with steep lines in multiple colors were suddenly everywhere. Many of us—not just scientists and computer whizzes—were comparing enormous numbers having to do with the populations of specific cities and countries to understand whether we would be affected by this mysterious and frightening disease. Data had suddenly become a matter of life and death.

Perhaps it's no surprise that data's importance burst onto the public stage because of concerns about health and well-being. Health care has been in the forefront of collecting and analyzing data for over a decade. If during your annual checkup your provider alternates between peppering you with questions and tapping into a computer, it's because health care in the last fifteen years has transitioned from paper to electronic records. You've probably logged onto a website associated with your doctor's office to make appointments online and look up your latest test results. The intention is that information collected from each visit can be shared quickly and easily among the various medical professionals—say, your general practitioner, your cardiologist, and your dermatologist—to make the best decisions for your care. Four major medical records companies now exist in the United States. All of us are in one or more of these data management systems.

The benefits of data collection and information sharing go beyond the individual patient and into what's called population health.

Dr. Gary Hamilton, CEO of InteliChart, a company that works with health care data all over the United States, estimates that his company processes about six hundred million patient transactions per month. InteliChart can't see any personal identifying information about individual patients (because of strict privacy regulations), but it can collect enormous amounts of information about large groups of patients to determine best health practices for the overall population. Interestingly, in analyzing this big data—and, yes, this is truly big data—Hamilton's company found that the most important contributor to the success of a medical intervention is not the actual treatment or therapy but the patient's socioeconomic background. A patient who is educated and in a stable job, has adequate transportation, and does not experience food insecurity will do much better than a patient who does not have those advantages.

The same predictions are true in education.

Like the health care industry, our system of education produces an enormous amount of information. We look to data for answers about why one student or school district is more successful than others and what factors influence gaps in student performance. Thanks to data, we now know that student learning outcomes are largely dependent on parents' income and education level; on whether the student is living in a stable home environment and is well nourished; on whether he or she has access to safe places to play; and to what extent, if any, he or she has suffered trauma. This is why understanding and nurturing the whole child is so crucial.

In the future, data will become increasingly important to education in at least two ways: to inform individualized learning and to drive district decision-making. The most effective teachers understand how to leverage student data to increase learning opportunities in the classroom. The highest-performing districts understand the necessity of collecting, analyzing, and using data.

To be clear: this chapter is not a how-to on using data or implementing big data. Nor is it an advertisement for any specific data platforms. Choosing a data collection and analytics platform should be based on specific school or district needs and budget. Instead, this chapter presents an overview of some of the basic kinds of data, provides insights from experts into the different ways that data can be used, and offers a peek into the future of data.

Keys to the Kingdom

Data is all around us. Many critical decisions affecting the learning environment—district operations; local, state, and federal reporting; individual student learning plans; resource planning; and more—can be made using reliable data. But what exactly are we talking about when we talk about data? The following are just a few basic types of data:

- **Quantitative data** refers to quantities: information that can be counted, measured, and expressed using numbers. Examples: your shoe size, standardized test scores, and the weather forecast.
- **Qualitative data** refers to qualities: descriptions and conceptualizations that cannot be expressed in numbers. Examples: the style of your shoe, how teachers feel about student performance, and how the weather forecast affects your weekend plans.
- **Perception data** is a type of qualitative data that consists of information that helps us understand people's various perceptions about a given situation. Example: data collected in a survey that asks people to assess specific factors affecting their well-being.
- **Predictive data** is information used to make predictions about future outcomes or events. Example: a calculation of how many lives might be saved in six weeks if everyone practiced social distancing during a pandemic.

Data affects our daily lives profoundly, whether we know it or not. Data is the reason that Facebook knows how to target us with advertisements that can be eerily accurate about our purchasing preferences. You can be sure that if an online service is free to the customer, then the customer is the product. What this means is that online companies sell the customer data they collect when we are online—our location, shopping habits, Google search history, and much, much more—to other organizations that then analyze and use that information, often for marketing purposes.

Data has become an incredibly valuable commodity.

Some databases do exist that are genuinely free to the user, however—for example, the system that stores call numbers in a public library. Museums are another nonprofit institution that often offer truly free access to digital images of art in their database collections.

EXPERT IM

Once data has been aggregated, it becomes much more powerful. It introduces the opportunity to perform things like predictive analytics and machine learning, the basis of AI. The data really are the keys to the kingdom. It's an enormous opportunity.

—Dr. Gary Hamilton
CEO, InteliChart

The twenty-first-century computer, which is capable of speedily processing astonishing amounts of quantitative data, has given rise to myriad applications of this data. In medicine, data is used to improve patient health or track disease incidence in the population. Weather predictions that prepare us for stormy or sunny days rely on data. Government census collects data about citizens to determine voting districts. Cities maintain data about crime to promote safety. Data is a fact of life. It's a compelling tool for seeing patterns and trends and making predictions. Before discussing how education can and will embrace data's opportunities, let's think about its promise and possibility by looking outward, beyond the world of education.

Location, Location, Location

Cell phone location data that's gathered from the mobile phones we all carry around these days is a huge data source with seemingly endless opportunities for use. Cell phones work by transmitting signals from your phone to the cell phone tower in nearest proximity, which then transmits the signal from tower to tower until it reaches the one closest to the person you are calling. Cell phone location data can be used to track disease patterns, traffic patterns, the habits of retail shoppers, and even criminal activities.

Polling Groups and Surveys

Polling groups, such as Gallup and Pew Research Group, collect valuable and fascinating perception data about current events. Political candidates and elected officials have long relied on polls and surveys to understand what citizens are thinking and feeling and to make forecasts about their electability.

Entertainment and Consumer Behavior Data

Netflix is a prime example of an online video streaming company that has invested enormous resources for the past couple of decades to become personal recommenders to its viewers. How does it do this? Every time you watch or even preview a movie on its site, the title goes into an enormous database that influences the next set of recommendations that Netflix shows you. In this way, you and the data you generate are interacting and learning from one another, which is a basic definition of artificial intelligence (AI). In the future, these types of human and machine interactions will become even more prevalent in our everyday lives.

It's time that we in education took better advantage of the opportunities for learning that data collection and data analysis offer. We're living in a world profoundly directed by data-driven technology. In many ways, data-informed education is also already upon us. It's a question of learning what data can and can't yet do, and how we can incorporate its lessons into our best practices.

Data-Informed Education

Classroom teaching already relies on the collection of data. Testing tracks students' proficiencies, analyzes their current ability, and tracks how much they've improved since the last testing period. Teachers gather fluency data for the children in their classes and keep running records on graded assignments throughout the year. Currently, we're better at gathering data in math, perhaps because it's easier to measure the discrete skills in mathematics than it is to measure the developmental approach of learning and utilizing language. I think we probably have a natural affinity, or at least more confidence, in applying numbers to kids when they're learning something more concrete and quantitative like math rather than something more abstract like English language arts.

School systems and districts have developed very sophisticated ways to match intervention supports with adaptive data. Reading instructors know that a child who needs to learn foundational reading using phonics or early comprehension strategies needs a different kind of support than a child who might be able to decode words but can't break down passages. Most districts across the country have been able to leverage adaptive assessment to determine that if a student has a certain risk score, they'll use a specific intervention.

On a district level, gathering the right data and analyzing it for commonalities are an opportunity to catch issues earlier and create earlier interventions. Union County School District in North Carolina, a very high performing school system, credits part of its success to the ability to use data as a framework for generating the key strategies they need for school and system improvement. Of course, collecting data is one thing, but figuring out what to do with it is essential. The district superintendent in Union County, Andrew G. Houlihan, offers this advice:

> One of the first steps is figuring out what your data is telling you. Where are your gaps? Where are your successes? What are those opportunities for improvement? How do you continue to put the foot on the gas to make sure that you're not letting up on the positive things that are happening for children? Let your data do the driving for you. It tells your story. It's factual; it's not opinion based.

The following are some things we in education can currently do with data: We can measure proficiency, especially in mathematics, and use data to inform interventions, especially in reading. At the district level, we can learn to read data to create early intervention opportunities and push positive improvement. But we're not where we need to be in education. We need to do more. What if we could monitor and track meaningful data about our students' individual learning and growth, compare it to that of their peers, and then direct them along the fastest and most efficient educational route?

Another thing that we can do well is collect perception data. This capability shouldn't be overlooked. Principals, superintendents, and other education administrators might tend to see the insights gleaned from perception polls as subjective, not "hard data." But this is a mistake.

Perception data can be a powerful predictor—if you know how to read it.

Perception Is Predictive

In late 2010, twenty-six-year-old Mohamed Bouazizi marched in front of a Tunisian government building and set himself on fire. Protests began that day, captured by cell phone cameras and shared on the internet. Within days, protests started popping up across Tunisia, calling for the ouster of President Zine El Abidine Ben Ali. A month later, he fled the country. The momentum that developed in Tunisia set off uprisings across the Middle East that became known as the Arab Spring. Within weeks, these uprisings had spread from Tunisia to Egypt, Yemen, Bahrain, Libya, and Syria. Millions of people of all ages and backgrounds flooded the streets to demand reform. Many observers around the world hoped that this uprising would bring in new governments that would deliver political reform and social justice. Optimism was high.

In December 2011, the Gallup organization polled people in Egypt about their views on various aspects of the Arab Spring. Gallup has been conducting surveys for seventy years. To understand what the world thinks about a particular issue, the organization polls thousands of people around the globe every single day. In late 2011, the new Egyptian leadership was issuing official reports to the world stating that their country was in great shape. The government claimed people were happy, that their demands had been met, and that finances were strong.

But the data from Gallup's perception polls showed a very different picture. People's perception of the situation was in fact the opposite. Surveys revealed that people felt that they were struggling; they felt that their community and financial well-being was floundering. Overall, the perception data demonstrated that the Egyptian people felt broken.

Much to the surprise of worldwide observers, this perception turned out to be predictive. By 2012, optimism for the Arab Spring began to crumble. The reality became more war and violence, and a crackdown on protesters. Five years later, human rights were under attack across the region. And today, conflicts continue to rage in Syria, Libya, and Yemen.

It's a tragic story, but it shows the power of perception data. Even though all looked great on the outside, the people on the streets of these countries understood and expressed a deeper truth. Their low level of well-being spoke to hidden systemic issues that were smoldering below the surface.

Surveys about well-being conducted in schools can be just as predictive as they are in geopolitics. In one specific instance, Gallup Education examined a large data pool it had collected at a school. The data showed that people's perception about their engagement, and thus performance, was high. But engagement, it turns out, is not as important to achievement as well-being—at least in this instance. Even though students' survey answers demonstrated high levels of engagement in schoolwork, their responses also demonstrated low levels of well-being. In the survey, the students said they didn't feel safe in their community. They didn't feel connected. They didn't feel good about their relationships.

Why is this important?

These student perceptions of poor well-being were soon followed by plummeting engagement scores. And these scores were soon followed by lower test and performance scores. The students' perceptions of well-being were thus a leading indicator of performance—the perception data was predictive. This data set also shows that well-being is more central to how well, or poorly, a school will do than is engagement. (Remember, it's about the whole child.) In a very straightforward way, we can develop a predictive chain of data from this example: well-being → engagement → performance.

The lesson? Pay attention to those student surveys. And when you see well-being scores fall, start planning interventions. Otherwise, you'll soon see engagement and performance follow suit. This is especially important in the aftermath of the COVID-19 pandemic and the civil unrest due to the killing of George Floyd. Once students return to school, whether in fall 2020 or spring 2021, they'll be dealing with significant amounts of anxiety and trauma. This is an instance in which the perception data on well-being is critical to making decisions and supporting students.

Tracking student well-being requires understanding what students might be going through outside the school walls, whether that is trauma or just plain family difficulties. In polling students, Gallup found five commonalities that drive an individual's sense of well-being:

- Do people have a sense of purpose every single day?
- Do they have meaningful relationships with one another and with their teachers?
- Are physical needs for food, sleep, and movement adequately met?
- Do they feel connected to something bigger than themselves?
- Do they feel safe?

In its polls, Gallup found that 70 percent of students thrive in one of these areas, but only 7 percent thrive in all five areas.[1]

Survey data is a starting point for deeper conversations and further analysis. Surveys that tell us what's happening at one point in time are a tool for figuring out how to respond as leaders and educators. Once you have the data that students are feeling lonely or disconnected or scared, the appropriate response very well may be to ask more questions—though not of the survey type. Rather, educators would need to engage in the kinds of conversations that take place when they ask authentic, caring questions to determine the state of well-being of all students.

Data-Driven Opportunities

On a district level, data analytics can help with very pragmatic problem solving. For example, technology can help leaders build master schedules that enable kids to have different-length periods. These schedules can allow more time for student engagement throughout the day or, for example, enable some students to spend thirty minutes on an algebra lesson while other students are given sixty or ninety minutes, depending on their learning needs. With so many variables involved, it's one thing to build a flexible school day if you have a system of two hundred students, but another, much more complicated thing to do with three hundred thousand students.

EXPERT IM

We want to develop and use analytics to help with pragmatic problem solving. How do you build supports in the school day? How do you better leverage your teaching staff? We're trying to take the numbers and suggest how districts—especially large districts—can solve these types of problems.

—David Bain
Vice president of academic planning & analytics, Houghton Mifflin Harcourt

Districts can also use data to interpret and predict important demographic trends in the area—for example, who's buying homes, how many families are homeless, or how many children are being born to single parents. The numbers that track these trends are rife with meaning for school leaders who learn how to pay attention.

Data analytics is crucial to how districts will understand and make decisions about budgets, what services to provide, how involved they'll need to be in the community, what level of interventions they'll need to provide, and much more. Schools are no longer just a place for students to memorize facts or consume knowledge. Schools exist within a community of families, and the health and wealth of those families has a lot to do with education needs and, ultimately, what goes on in the classroom between teachers and kids.

Without quantitative demographic data, superintendents and other high-level education leaders are reduced to using guesswork, intuition, and past successes, which although appropriate in some contexts, are not in themselves reliable tools for the consequential decision-making that affects large populations. Quantitative data, when properly analyzed and intelligently understood, is a powerful informant to the very human decisions that leaders must inevitably make about whom they serve.

We know we can collect test data about math and reading skills, but what about social and emotional learning, the so-called soft skills? The future holds promise for that too. According to Shauna McDonald, the executive director of Playworks in Minnesota, an organization called Reflection Sciences and the University of Minnesota have developed an executive functioning scale that measures social-emotional competence (https://reflectionsciences.com). This is the only measurement of SEL capabilities we have that's valid and cost effective. With this tool, educators have begun to measure where students are on the spectrum of executive functioning. Understanding this is important to inform a whole-child approach to learning and to priming students for long-term success. With this newer measurement, as McDonald told me, we're "right on the cusp of really understanding that in early childhood, not just preK but up through elementary school, if we make an investment in measuring and supporting social and emotional learning, it will pay off later." This early investment would lessen the burden and cost to educators in middle and high schools, who now face the difficult challenge of having to triage kids who lack SEL skills needed to succeed at higher academic levels.

The Data "Dream"

With advances in data collection and data analytics, we're starting to see what are called *connected teaching platforms.* These platforms collect assessment data and provide real-time pedagogical suggestions to teachers. This is the dream of all data professionals in education—a unified platform that assesses students during lessons and activities, then cues teachers to the best content or learning strategies to use with an individual student or a certain group of students. Teachers would be able to see what types of content other teachers selected when they came across similar students with similar challenges. What were typical growth or response rates? Did the sequence matter? Perhaps most important, the assessment system wouldn't operate outside regular learning but in conjunction with the learning.

Just consider, if a teacher has 150 students, she may not be able to determine some of the underlying reasons that, for example, learning algebra is so difficult for one particular child. But this type of technology could assist the teacher by figuring out that the child's difficulty is due to a fundamental misunderstanding of a critical concept that should have been learned years earlier. The teacher might be able to discover this same thing with very careful questioning strategies, but it would be time consuming and would take away from time spent with the other 149 students. This speaks to one of the major hurdles to incorporating innovative learning strategies in the classroom: teachers are often asked to do too many time-consuming tasks. I believe that teachers shy away from some of the most highly effective instructional strategies at least partly because of the downstream burden it places on them. The data that a connected teaching platform provides could alleviate this burden and free up teachers for the creative and relational work that we know is central to the classroom.

Ultimately, the goal for a unified platform is ongoing data collection that doesn't just chart students but also offers meaningful interventions. The hope is to be able to collect data both formally and through informal reporting. When a child is playing an online education game, we want to be able to informally assess skills along the way in order to create a more complete and robust learning profile. This type of adaptive assessment might occur three times a year. But it could also be conducted on a random day of the week, when the child is working on an assignment at home, or at night, or while he or she is playing an online game. Then this type of informal assessment could guide the teacher in determining the next day's lesson.

Much of the technology is already here, and we know it can be used in ways that respect and support teachers' core strengths. What's lagging is our comfort level and the adoption of a mindset that embraces the opportunities created by data. In nearly every industry, there's been an enormous amount of initial pushback when leaders have introduced data management technology. The same is true in education. Like so many changes, adoption of data analytics requires trust. Use of this technology can require learning new skills, processes, and mindsets. Educators—like health care professionals or financial analysts or entertainment executives—will in time see the very real ways in which data collection, management, and analysis can transform their work and improve the lives of the students they serve.

Data will individualize student learning in much the same ways that health data has individualized patient health. We're already beginning to do this with Lexile scores, as discussed in the previous chapter. We're seeing some EdTech firms and publishing companies take small steps toward creating these types of integrated systems, especially in math. A well-incorporated, unified platform is clearly in our future. It will come much quicker for some districts than for others. I believe that when a few districts operationalize the use of such data, the demand for its use in all districts will be pushed by the political community, parents, and the media. Eventually, we'll have these types of systems for math, reading, and even for secondary disciplines such as science and social studies. And when we do, they will truly change the way our classrooms operate.

Despite these many and marvelous data-driven opportunities—to individualize student learning, facilitate large-scale scheduling, and assist demographically informed decisions—there are limits to what even the best data can do. Data is not always perfect; it doesn't always provide the answer. Data has its downsides, too.

Not the Be-All, End-All

There are limits to what we can capture with data. The important skills that make us uniquely human are difficult—though not impossible—to measure. More to the point, technology will never replace meaningful human interactions and relationships. The most sophisticated data analysis won't teach people how to collaborate with one another, create something truly new and beautiful, or care about the well-being of a community. Instead, we need to teach people how to *leverage* technology and information in their interactions, in data simulations, and in problem solving. How do you use technology to visualize large data sets? How do you think about and analyze the data you've collected? How do you communicate your findings to others?

In the end, we need to keep in mind that data is just a snapshot of any given moment. Many of us may be overly fixated on data and its promise, partly because some people use data to prove their success. We know we're a great school or a great district because the numbers show it! In this way, we reduce meaningful data to a point of comparison, rather than use it as a guide for improvement. Many of us also tend to overcomplicate data. If we're measuring, say, engagement, we devise twenty data points. When engagement comprises twenty different things, it's impossible to design and implement meaningful interventions. In this case, there is just too much data with too many variables. In these ways, data can become a broken lens—a snapshot that doesn't actually help us improve day-to-day outcomes.

EXPERT IM

Data can inform some things, but not all things. We still need to design powerful learning opportunities that support connection and creativity. I don't think technology can teach those skills.

—Karen Cator
President and CEO, Digital Promise

One of the challenges with education is that we have to allow the data to suggest and guide rather than dictate particular methods. We need to respect teachers' identity. A core benefit of teachers is the talents they possess to curate the learning experience based on their knowledge of child development and the relationships they've built with their students. Because of this, I believe that the most powerful technologies in the future will resemble virtual teaching assistants that can monitor progress and suggest strategies, while still granting the true power, the choice of the learning experience, to the educator in the room.

At the end of the day, data collection and analysis are not infallible. They are only part of the bigger picture. Human beings still need to make decisions using judgment and experience. And when these decisions are made, we as leaders still need to convince, cajole, and inspire others to put them into action. Decisions without action are pointless.

Turn Data into Action

A quick question: Three frogs sit on a log. One decides to hop off. How many frogs are left?

Before you answer, let me give you a clue: a decision is not the same as an action. Deciding to buy a house—or write a novel or start a business—is completely different than doing the work needed to enact that decision. The same is true of data; it can provide us with information, open our eyes, and inform our decisions, but we still need to take action. Otherwise, it's meaningless.

The answer to my question, of course, is that three frogs are left on the log.

We as leaders need to know how to act. The best data collection and most insightful data analysis are useless unless we act on the findings. This is especially true when it comes to opinion polls and surveys. We need to be careful—and responsible—with how we handle this type of data. If we keep asking students questions but then fail to convert the answers into meaningful interventions, they'll feel as though their opinions don't matter. Then, when the next set of survey questions comes around, students won't provide authentic, meaningful answers. And this, we know, triggers a decrease in engagement—followed by declining performance.

All educators must commit to turning data into action. Data analysis is a tool not only for education administrators and leaders but for all stakeholders. Even though we can collect a significant amount of data, many teachers aren't sure how to build lesson plans around numbers, statistics, trends, or other findings. It takes practice and skill to assess student data and ask the right questions. According to the numbers, what's the most appropriate content? What's the most appropriate instruction plan? Which students should be grouped together to participate in a specific experience? These types of questions can lead to confusion and even paralysis. It's part of a school leader's job to help teachers learn how to translate data into action.

Collaborating with peers in professional learning communities to dissect and understand data and reflect on collective strengths and weaknesses that the data reveals is one way to develop curriculum that best serves the needs of classrooms and schools. For guidance with practical, step-by-step implementations of data, take a look at chapter 7 (Support Decision Making with Data Systems) in my book *The Daggett System for Effective*

Instruction. The website for ICLE—https://leadered.com/—is another terrific resource for learning more about data, data analytics, and data-driven decision-making.

LESSONS FOR THE FUTURE

- Data—quantitative, qualitative, perception, and predictive—is all around us. A close analysis of data benefits us because we can use it to inform individualized learning in the classroom, drive district decision-making, and support student growth.
- Perception data is more powerful than many of us realize. The data collected through surveys and polls can predict the direction of a school or district.
- Data analytics can help education leaders with pragmatic problem solving—such as class or school scheduling—and make predictions about future demographics that drive school- or district-level decisions.
- The dream is to create a connected, integrated assessment and learning platform that facilitates individualized learning. Ongoing informal assessment in this type of integrated system can act as a virtual assistant to teachers, offering optimized learning interventions. We've taken small steps toward creating this type of connected data platform, but we're not there yet.
- There are limits to what data can capture. It's a snapshot in time that shows only one part of a bigger picture. To make good decisions, we still need human judgment and interpretation. Even when this snapshot is accurate and the data properly interpreted, what we have learned must always be followed with action. Without action, data is pointless.

8

The Classroom of the Future

We've reached a tipping point.

Because of COVID-19, the schools and classrooms of the future are happening *right now.* In a matter of weeks, K–12 education in the US and around the world was forced to shift to distance and remote learning. As of May 2020, school closures in over 160 countries had separated nearly 87 percent of the world's student population from their peers and teachers. In the United States alone, more than fifty-five million students were attempting to learn from home.[1]

Teachers scrambled to get content online, to connect with their students virtually, and to bring a little bit of regularity back into everyone's life. Administrators and support staff came up with creative solutions for distributing meals and learning packets to students in need. Meanwhile, parents—many of whom are understanding for the first time how difficult it is to work from home *and* support their child's learning—struggled to adapt to their new reality.

Have parents ever valued teachers and schools as much as they do now? Probably not. This is a testament to the fact that today's educators are far from "failing," but rather are real-world heroes who should be celebrated and applauded. Consider that with the flip of a switch, they went from teaching thirty students in a classroom to trying to reach, console, and influence thirty students in thirty different locations through digital devices. The controlled, neat classroom was fractured, and faithful lesson plans discarded. It has been a challenge for all of us.

There have been positives in this experience. We know that because of its availability, its accessibility, its reach, and its cost savings, this type of distance learning is a significant part of the future. Business communication platforms such as Zoom have been turned into learning platforms, effective for discussion and feedback. We know that students can share project results and collaborate remotely. Many of these are concepts or mediums that have been discussed, projected, and hoped for, but never tested or implemented on a large scale. We've now seen that we can incorporate them—even when we're in panic mode. In this way, the pandemic has accelerated the use of technology in education.

But, sadly, it has also amplified many of the problems with education.

As schools shifted almost entirely online, one of our first realizations was how technology underscores many existing inequities in education. While affluent parents hired tutors and created their own learning communities, other families had more basic concerns, such as hunger, unemployment, and homelessness. Think about the tools children need in order to participate in digital learning: they must have a device that can access the internet and a high-speed internet connection, and—depending on their age—they may need assistance from a parent, guardian, or caregiver. This seems simple enough. But the truth is that nearly twelve million American students lack access to the internet at home. Some may only have access on their phone, making them unable to complete all of their schoolwork. Others live in rural areas and lack adequate internet or cellular service. And still others are among the 1.3 million students experiencing homelessness in our country.[2] Add to this the millions of English language learners, and you can see the colossal challenge in front of us.

As many in our nation sheltered at home, some teachers have reported that only 20 percent of their students have been logging on for lessons.[3] That leaves a majority of their class missing out on valuable learning and socialization. By the time our students return to the classroom, they may have missed months of instruction. These are gaps in education and development that will be difficult to make up. This is a real concern that we need to address before we can move toward the future. And in many ways this is a policy issue that involves funding, social priorities, and infrastructure development. But that doesn't change the fact that we as educators still need to be cognizant of inequity in order to better plan for the future.

We must commend educators for their amazing efforts in the midst of the crisis. But it has also become clear that for many children, virtual classrooms are inaccessible—or simply not a priority right now. We know that online and remote learning has its shortcomings. This doesn't mean that technology isn't an integral part of the evolution of education. It does mean that we need to rethink our priorities. Technology won't replace the humanistic qualities that are essential to teaching; if anything, this experience has highlighted how valuable they are. So how do we begin to address these challenges? To start, we need to reaffirm our commitment to change.

No More Excuses

When will we get back to normal? Never. We're never going back to the past. We have a new normal. And this new normal means that we're out of excuses. We educators have to change how our students learn if we're going to give them the best chances for success in our technology-driven, globalized economy. We have to change if we want to rebuild our historically strong economy, which has brought prosperity to more of us throughout society than has that of any other nation in history. We have to change if we want to continue to provide benefits and support to our fellow citizens in need. And we have to change if we hope to fund both equity and excellence in public education so that ALL children in our country can fulfill their potential.

The education industry and we as individual educators have to change. We can no longer tolerate a situation where it's nearly impossible to change things as simple as the bell schedule or school calendar. Together, we must decide that accepting these practices and systems as "facts" is no longer part of our culture, our vision, or our mindset as twenty-first-century educators. Our "business as usual" can no longer be business as usual—it must evolve.

And this change starts with us.

We as leaders must become more nimble, flexible, innovative, and capable, just as we're asking our students to do. We must do this so that we can be the leaders and agents of change our communities so desperately need. And we must do this so that we can begin to create more flexible and innovative classrooms, schools, and districts that meet the future needs of our students and provide equity for ALL.

There is an immense benefit to becoming more nimble, innovative educators who work in more nimble, innovative schools and districts. By doing so, we mirror these skills to our students. They too will need these capabilities to survive and thrive in an uncertain, hypercompetitive world. As the oft-quoted adage goes, "Be the change you want to see in the world."[4] If we embody these skills ourselves, we will more naturally incorporate learning them into our curriculum, lesson plans, and extracurricular activities. We'll also familiarize our students with working and learning in modern, more relevant settings, just like the ones most of them are likely to work in one day. We must walk the walk. And if there's one thing that we learned during the pandemic, it's the importance of thinking of our students—of their health and well-being—first.

The Whole Child Comes First

When the pandemic struck, what was the initial concern for many educators? Was it standardized tests? No. Was it getting books and assignments to students? No. Educators' initial concern was focused on such issues as how to feed all the kids who face food scarcity and how to meet the needs of special education students.

First and foremost, educators were concerned with the well-being of their students. They wanted to make sure children had nutritious meals, both to maintain their physical health and to create at least a slight sense of normality. In the wake of school shutdowns, educators found many creative ways to check in: sending text messages, personalized videos, or even driving through students' neighborhoods with signs that read, "I miss you." As discussed in chapter 3, the social and emotional health of our students has become a core responsibility for our schools.

Our narrow focus on content—passing the next test, achieving the next grade level—is not enough. Sadly, we've seen the consequences of emphasizing academics over everything else. The mental health crisis among our children is staggering. As I pointed out in chapter 1, rates of anxiety and depression have skyrocketed. In the past, we lost sight of the whole child. In the post-2020 world, this is not acceptable. We now understand that fostering students' mental health is an essential part of educating ALL children.

EXPERT IM

Engagement is 100 percent emotional. Say a child has a best friend at school and a teacher who cares about him or her as a person. Those are really the top reasons children want to go to school. If you combine

> those top two reasons, they'll show up at school because they get to see their best friend and they get to be authentically cared for.
>
> —Katie Lyon
> Managing director, higher education, Gallup

Before the pandemic struck, it was estimated that more than 60 percent of students had experienced some kind of trauma, such as hunger, domestic violence, divorce, transiency, or homelessness.[5]

Well, that number is now nearly 100 percent.

During the break, our students have been faced with larger concerns than schoolwork: Will my loved ones get sick? How am I supposed to complete my schoolwork and take care of my younger siblings? What if I don't feel safe at home? With the recent disruptions to the school year, identifying and helping the most vulnerable students has become more complex and multifaceted. Unfortunately, these circumstances are the new normal. Much like issues with inequity, these are challenges that students and educators must face every day—except that now we need to add a new anxiety to the list. We have to worry not only about school shootings and bullying but also about our children spending time in a single, closed space with thirty other sneezing, coughing people. Add biological hazard to the list of concerns that make students feel unsafe at school. And because so many children face trauma at home, school is both a place to escape trauma—and a place with increased trauma.

Moving forward, students who struggled with a typical curriculum and with forming trust will need intentional plans to meet their mental health needs and their need for social and emotional learning. They'll also need time to rebuild relationships—now the first of the three R's in the Rigor/Relevance Framework—with educators. For those suffering the most acute forms of trauma, the need to address the first R will be a critical challenge, especially as online and remote learning becomes more common.

Learning—and Caring—beyond School

School is a social space where students interact and form relationships with their teachers and peers. In the absence of face-to-face interactions, how do we continue to create meaningful connections? As it turns out, it's difficult to do this over Zoom or FaceTime. Technology often increases feelings of loneliness. Even though kids these days are glued to their smartphones, constantly in touch with their friends, that doesn't mean they experience deep, meaningful relationships. Add to this that they are now unable to see their friends and family members in person—unable to attend graduation or participate in team sports. This creates fertile ground for feelings of isolation, desperation, and even hopelessness.

But how do you teach SEL virtually? How do you facilitate organized play over a video stream? This is especially relevant now, when educators interact with students from afar. We're all just a face on the other end of a network, separated by miles of space and limited by digital latency. We can tell our students that we care about them. We assure them that we'll see them soon. But we can't manage the culture or the learning environment around them. We can't oversee play or teach to a moment. We're a face on a screen; a single influence in a wave of anxiety and confusion. As we now know, it's much harder—though not impossible—to create the nurturing, supportive culture of a well-organized, effective classroom through an online portal.

Can we really develop these kinds of relationships with our students online? Can we address their emotional and physical well-being through an email or a text message? SEL issues are deeply embedded within technology. It was apparent before the pandemic, and it's even more obvious now: students experiencing stressors in their life have difficulty participating—much less excelling—in their schoolwork. Without regular contact hours in the classroom, teachers will find it difficult to get in touch with some, or even many, of their students. Yes, we're more connected than ever before, yet we find ourselves longing for community and more authentic relationships. And this may be one of the keys to making remote learning feel a little less remote: moving from a focus on the whole child to a focus on the whole family.

From the Whole Child to the Whole Family

Although we've always known that families are central to effective learning, recent events have made them more vital than ever before. For this reason, we as school leaders need to take our whole-child thinking even one step further: we need to start thinking about the whole family. I discuss the idea of community schools in depth in chapter 4, but it's a message worth repeating.

A community school provides medical and mental health care, legal counseling for families, food, clothing, and many other necessities. Through community partnerships, community schools can also address achievement by offering additional academic support such as tutoring, field trips, and internship opportunities with local businesses and organizations. After the school day is finished, the building doesn't need to shutter. Instead, it can continue to serve as a meeting space for families and community members.

The goal is to expand services that support students' academic achievement, address their physical and mental health, and offer more convenient ways for families to connect with the school. Research has shown that when students feel safe and connected to their community, they're more likely to be engaged at school. The same goes for their parents. In many ways, this is an investment in families as instructional partners and direct participants in school culture. And although we may be forced to distance ourselves, there will come a time when we return to this school culture, to the physical learning space.

The New—and the Old

The classroom of the future is blended. Technology is a necessity in today's world, and students need to be comfortable using it for their future jobs. After rapidly transitioning to remote learning, we can see even more clearly that our schools must evolve in a way that effectively incorporates technology into the learning process. Embracing new tools in the classroom can help relieve teachers of certain time-consuming tasks, such as tracking and grading, and help them move toward teaching the skills needed for the future.

We saw this change taking place even before COVID-19. Online education courses were popping up across the country, and a number of public schools had begun adopting online curricula to create a more individualized learning experience. There are plenty of electronic platforms, with more coming as companies create new systems to drive learning. In conjunction with all this, many school districts are working with publishers and online education companies to change how instructional materials and learning resources are developed and delivered. Each of these tools and resources deserves educators' attention. Each has the potential to increase rigor and engagement for ALL learners. But in the end, they're only tools—conduits for learning. To be truly effective, to reach the whole child, they need to be joined with proven, time-tested learning strategies.

Old Wisdom—New Technologies

We live in a moment when there's nonstop hype around innovation in education or the reimagining of education. We hear various ideas recycled over and over again—online courses, personalized learning, a tablet with advanced educational apps in every child's hands. The catchphrases are even worse—"disrupt the system," "break things fast and innovate," "doing something (anything!) is better than doing nothing." Some opt for radical solutions with little evidence that any of them work. Often, these ideas are accompanied by dire economic scenarios that lay the entire hope of our economy at the feet of school administrators, principals, and teachers. Talk about pressure!

Yes, we do need to adapt to the changing global economy. If you've read this far into the book, you already know this. But it should also be clear that, as we have learned during the pandemic, technology and innovation have their limitations. We now know that hurried or rushed implementation leads to more problems than it solves.

Therefore, the first step in creating effective and engaging blended learning is, as author Weston Kieschnick writes, to "pump the brakes on innovation."[6] That's right. To better innovate, we need to slow down. We need to pause, catch our breath, and think through many of the issues discussed in this chapter and throughout this book. We need to get a realistic picture of today—and a realistic vision for tomorrow. We're all trying to juggle rapid change at the moment, but we need to keep our eye on 2025, 2028, or even 2030. Kieschnick's book *Bold School: Old School Wisdom + New School Technologies = Blended Learning That Works* is a great place to learn more about how to develop and implement powerful blended learning strategies.

One of his key points about blended learning is that "what works works, with or without technology."[7] In other words, technology needs to be used to support and assist effective learning strategies, not replace them. With this in mind, Kieschnick supplies the following simple five-step framework for designing and implementing successful blended learning:

1. Identify desired academic outcome(s).
2. Select a goal-aligned instructional strategy that *works.*
3. Choose digital tool(s).
4. Plan blended instruction.
5. Self-assess your plans and progress with a framework.

This approach puts proven learning strategies first, then considers what technological tools may work best to support these strategies. It also aligns with the Rigor/Relevance Framework I described in chapter 4 and discuss in detail in my book *Rigor, Relevance, and Relationships in Action.* Through this approach, we avoid discarding what we've discovered about effective learning just so we can fit a new shiny tablet or laptop into the classroom.

Learning Takes Place Anywhere, Anytime

This type of "learning first, tech tools second" approach enables us as experienced educators to combine proven learning techniques with technological solutions. This approach is a means of using technology to better challenge our students, one that's very different from that of the traditional "sage on the stage"—in which the teacher lectures for an entire period—that's found in some classrooms.

This is particularly important now that we know that blended learning has come to include remote and asynchronous learning. As we move toward the future, we as educators need to be ready to shift on the fly from in-person to remote instruction. The pandemic has taught us that although we understand and appreciate the value of the classroom, we can't be tethered to it. We must be able to transfer effective learning strategies to online platforms. By necessity, the truly blended classroom includes effective strategies for teaching both inside and outside the classroom. Approached this way, orienting to remote learning isn't only about the medium of instruction; it's actually about building and unleashing more student-centered, individualized learning for students, no matter the medium. If we apply proven strategies with new tools, then effective learning can take place anywhere, anytime—during stable times or during a crisis.

When the education world went completely online in 2020, there was a lot of speculation from technology advocates and futurists that this interruption would change everything. All learning was remote learning. And it's true, the events of 2020 changed everything—but not exactly in the way most futurists had hoped. From talking with hundreds of school leaders and innovative educators, I came away with the sense that the opposite realization took hold: the widespread separation of students and teachers has actually showed us how irreplaceable the classroom is to learning, especially equitable learning.

Tomorrow's Classroom

There will always be a place in education for great teaching. Research from experts like John Hattie is clear: teachers have the single most significant impact on student outcomes. Will AI have a role in education? Absolutely. Data analytics and automation? Yes and yes. But I don't believe that machines or software will ever take the place of a classroom teacher. And by extension, schools and classrooms will be more important now—and in the future—than ever before.

Few people have advocated for technology in education more than I have. But I've always been a bit skeptical of arguments that learning will get better if we let technology disrupt the relationship between teachers and students. And far from taking all course work online, the coming decade will see both teachers and students returning to classrooms with renewed enthusiasm. It's every educator's dream: students will be thrilled to get back to school.

It is my hope that we educators will return with a renewed commitment to unlocking the power of good teaching practices and a supportive school culture. To me, schools and classrooms are first and foremost a microcosm of society that teaches students how to collaborate, empathize, and be good citizens. We can try to transmit these lessons across the internet, but many social and emotional self-management skills can only be taught—and safely experienced—in our classrooms. I believe that as we incorporate more technology in education, the classroom experience itself will become more humanistic, more focused on individual relationships and social connection.

Online learning still faces many obstacles, including the difficulty of teaching SEL, increased digital inequality, increased loneliness, and a lack of engagement. According to studies done by Gallup Education, engagement is one of the biggest problems for students participating in online learning. How do we capture and maintain students' interest? How do we motivate them to stick with a difficult topic or class? Without the culture and rigor of the classroom, students too easily drift away from challenging work or hard subjects. To counter these weaknesses in online learning, schools and classrooms will need to build on human connection, human relationships, and individual relevance.

EXPERT IM

Technology can and should be used as a facilitator of learning, but it will never replace the teacher who is there to make sure that learning happens.

—Dr. Andrew G. Houlihan
Superintendent of Union County School District, North Carolina

Many of the leaders in education whom I spoke with agreed that the best way to merge technology and the classroom is by shifting the focus to students first and foremost, not to content. Once upon a time, we looked toward massive open online courses (MOOCs) as the classrooms of the future, a boundless digital space where millions of people could learn. These types of courses do offer opportunities to learn, and will continue to exist. They have their place. But what we've actually seen unfolding recently is a move in the opposite direction. As AI, data analytics, and automation take over some tasks of teaching (e.g., grading, scheduling, and certain types of assessments), we'll see that teachers themselves will become more important. Our attention will be on relationships and authentically caring for one another.

Through this process, K–12 schools will begin to incorporate more project-based and self-directed learning. The high school of the future will focus more on making students career ready, rather than preparing them for higher education or a specific trade. This includes more focus on entrepreneurial aspirations, financial literacy, and applied learning. These shifts could have an effect on the traditional hours of a school day and the length of class periods. As I noted in an earlier chapter, it's possible to use technology to build master schedules that are specific to individual students' learning needs. This flexibility could also boost students' engagement, as they won't need to choose between, for example, music and math. Individualized schedules could also offer AM or PM classes, or even- and odd-day schedules, which would accommodate distance and remote learning, as necessary.

We need to continue down this path of letting technology do what it does best—increasing access, personalizing instruction, and allowing students to work at their own pace. In turn, teachers will be freed to do what they do best—strengthen relationships, encourage individuals, and support the development of personal and interpersonal skills. This will go a long way toward helping create productive, conscientious, and engaged citizens, not to mention highly sought-after employees. But it will also require teachers to embrace new roles in the classroom.

New Goals, New Roles

Have you ever heard statements like these: "I just wanted to teach biology" or "I got into this to teach kids how to read"? These types of objections are usually responses to the growing responsibilities of teachers: they're now asked to be instructors, counselors, motivators, and IT experts. There was a time when lecturing, assigning homework, and grading exams were enough to fulfill the job. But the future classroom requires teachers to do more than just perform a set of actions in front of students.

As our lives have fundamentally changed, the role of teachers in a child's education—and in American culture—has also changed. Instruction rarely consists of lecturing to students who sit at desks, dutifully listening. The trend away from this kind of teaching will continue over the next two, three, or five years. As we move deeper into the 2020s, teachers will be expected to offer every child a rich, rewarding, and unique learning experience. The day-to-day job of a teacher, rather than one of broadcasting content, will be one of designing engaging learning opportunities and guiding students through them. Information is no longer found primarily in books; it's available everywhere on phones, tablets, and other digital devices. This will help teachers create blended experiences that extend into the home and into the community. The following are four new roles that teachers must fulfill to be successful in the future:

- Social and emotional learning counselor
- Relationship builder
- Facilitator of learning
- EdTech specialist

A number of these roles have been touched on in previous chapters. In some cases, an entire chapter is devoted to a specific role. It's still helpful, though, to review each within the context of the future school and classroom.

Social and Emotional Learning Counselor

Educators will need to be well versed in social and emotional learning (SEL) and capable of supporting underserved or traumatized students. I discussed SEL in great depth in chapter 3, but I want to reiterate its importance in our postpandemic environment. The reality is, our world is getting less predictable, and the rate of change is so fast that our young people are often left feeling anxious and alone. Not to mention that there are real threats out there, such as school shootings and pandemics, that affect the safety and mental health of our students. Teachers will need to manage the social and emotional needs of their students and help them process their trauma in healthy ways. These skills will be crucial in unlocking students' potential and will often hinge on a teacher's ability to develop meaningful relationships with students.

Relationship Builder

As discussed in chapter 4, strong relationships make relevance and rigor possible. Therefore, teachers will need to be better at building relationships with students, other educators, parents, and the community. We're all human beings, and human beings are relational. We want to feel seen and cared for, and to know that we belong. Our students are no different, which is why it's critical that educators develop their skills of individualized perception—the ability to understand what makes a student tick and ask him authentic, caring questions to better understand his circumstances and reveal his personal passions. It's not so much about the intellect of the student; it's about creating an emotional connection, which allows the educator to come up with creative, individualized solutions for each student.

The need for these types of relationships extends beyond the classroom walls to coworkers and supervisors, as well as to families and the community. Maintaining healthy lines of communication and collaboration is essential if we want to help students thrive. This attention to personal qualities is all the more important as America continues to become the most pluralistic nation in the world. Teachers have to be committed to relating to students who represent many cultures. Only by creating these types of relationships can teachers truly become leaders of student learning.

Facilitator of Learning

We know from cognitive research that if you learn something on your own, you're significantly more likely to remember it. But if you learn it just to regurgitate it back to a teacher, you probably won't retain it for very long. Rather than lecturing from the front of the class, educators need to shift their focus toward facilitating the learning process. There are more ways to learn today than ever before. If you need to fix a specific problem, you can go on YouTube and find a video that walks you through the process. Our students know this; they're already skilled at using technology to find answers. This is why we need to shift from a system focused on teaching to a system focused on learning. Teachers will find that they accomplish more if they adopt the role of educational guide, facilitator, and even colearner. Instead of asking themselves, "How do I teach this specific content?" they'll reframe the question as, "How will my students learn this?"

Why is this framing so important? As I mentioned in multiple chapters throughout this book, students need to become lifelong learners capable of acquiring new skills, jumping from job to job, and working online or in person. Our best teachers will discover how to transform students into these types of passionate, self-directed learners by providing participatory educational adventures. To encourage students to truly take responsibility for their own education, the curriculum must relate to their lives, learning activities must engage their natural curiosity, and assessments must measure real accomplishments, not just seemingly arbitrary standards. In the classrooms of the future, the teacher's job will be managing individualized learning, as opposed to preparing students for tests. This means that teachers will need to have a solid grasp of technology and how to use it to support proven learning strategies.

EdTech Specialist

In the future, embracing technology will require more than being able to set up a Zoom account. Being tech savvy will entail blending the in-person and digital learning realms. Our future teachers must be able to collaborate, communicate, learn (engage in professional development), and care (nurture relationships) through technology. The old model of instruction was predicated on information scarcity. Teachers and their books were information oracles, spreading knowledge to a population with few other ways to get it. That paradigm will continue to change as technology evolves and connected learning platforms become more available.

EXPERT IM

From the perspective of a teacher, we're asking them to change what they've been doing for years. We're asking them to change their standards. We're asking them to change how they teach to those new standards. And we're asking them to be more involved with students in a meaningful way. This is a significant transition.

—MaryEllen Elia
ICLE senior partner and former commissioner of education of the state of New York

Maybe surprisingly, this paradigm shift also demands that we as leaders change how we approach technology in education. In studying how aptly new technology is applied in the classroom, Gallup Education found that most teachers don't feel as if they've been authorized to be creative in their teaching techniques. On the flipside, the more encouraged teachers feel to experiment and innovate, the more likely they will be to implement technology in the classroom. And this implementation directly leads to increased student engagement. The lesson? The more we as leaders implement technology and get teachers comfortable with how to use it, the more empowered they will feel to employ new, more engaging learning techniques.

This is important to understand. In redefining and reinventing the roles of teachers, we're asking for substantial changes in the way tasks are done both inside and outside the classroom. But teachers shouldn't be expected to shoulder this burden on their own. As we make these structural changes, districts and schools need to assist educators by offering quality professional learning opportunities that embolden and empower them.

Reteaching the Teachers

Looking forward, we know that teachers will need to better support student SEL, especially as anxiety increases in an uncertain world. We know that teachers will need to be better at building relationships and creating individualizing learning. And we know that teachers will need to be more effective at incorporating technology both inside the classroom and beyond the walls of the school. This is a lot to ask of already overwhelmed educators. To better support our teachers in making this transition toward the future, we as leaders must rethink some of our basic premises about what constitutes professional development.

State and municipal budgets are already suffering from reduced revenue. Due to these shortfalls, many districts are likely to be hesitant to fund professional development programs in the future—at least not traditional programs. Therefore, more innovative approaches must be found to deliver increasingly important developmental help. In my opinion, this new training will revolve around three significant changes: resiliency training to help with "emotional labor," training designed to close the technology gap, and improved modeling of successful learning strategies. Let's take a closer look at each of these changes.

Ease Emotional Labor

Emily Kaplan, a freelance journalist and former elementary school teacher, once made her entire second-grade class cry. She didn't do it intentionally. While giving a lesson on specific details in writing, she offered an example of how she'd felt after her grandmother died: she felt sad, she cried, and she sought comfort from her cat. This example set off an unexpected reaction in her students: they all started crying too, as they remembered loved ones they'd lost. Instead of continuing with her lesson, Kaplan found herself having to pivot and care for her students' emotions.[8]

This is the emotional labor that's required of teachers—and it's rarely included in the job description. As Kaplan explains, teaching is about "reaching clear to the heart of another human being and using everything you've got to make a difference. It's calming kids when they've had a rough recess, celebrating when they lose their first tooth, absorbing their struggles and their traumas, channeling their joy, and investing the currency of your own emotions in an effort to help them grow." Teachers must do this for all their students, even as they try to manage their own emotions. As teachers take greater responsibility for student mental and emotional well-being, we need to provide them with the types of resiliency training—the tools and knowledge—they need to care for themselves. Otherwise, the job can become soul crushing.

Close the Tech Gap

As we move toward the future, our professional development for teachers must be more extensive than a one-day class on how to use technology. This is clearly not sufficient. Teachers who are reluctant to adopt new technologies in their classroom have valid concerns, such as lack of time, resources, or confidence in their abilities. There's also a learning gap between those teachers who aren't as comfortable with technology and teachers who will readily adopt the latest digital tool. This is why technology needs to be an integral part of our plans for personal growth. Instructional technology specialists say that ideally teachers should receive weeks or even months of training on how to use online learning programs.

At the same time, it's important to realize that technology has opened the doors of the classroom, allowing teachers to learn from each other and share best practices. It's easier than ever to access massive amounts of information on our smartphones and computers. Likewise, it's easier to share information with people all over the world. This has created new opportunities to communicate and collaborate. A classroom in Texas can connect with a classroom in Japan. A teacher giving a lesson on water quality can invite a scientist to give a virtual presentation to his or her students. The classroom is no longer confined to a physical space, to the four walls around it. Professional collaboration can be fostered through data teams, integrated curriculum, team teaching, project-based learning, and other models. This team approach encourages the use of shared resources and responsibilities, and dedicated, multitiered support systems. We need to optimize the openness of technology and foster more interaction among educators, other professionals, and the rest of the world.

Model Outcomes

In delivering these professional learning experiences either remotely or in person, facilitators must model the practices that schools would like to see teachers employ themselves. This is especially true when it comes to the use of technology. We increasingly expect teachers to incorporate technology in their classrooms, yet we rely on the same well-worn classroom-based techniques for training them. This usually involves sticking an old lesson plan into PowerPoint, then considering it forward thinking. We can do better.

Likely gone are the days of planning professional learning for just a couple of days a year and without educator input or meaningful follow-up. And it's not just that these one-off sessions have become ineffective—they've become irrelevant. Greater intentionality and preparation will be key in providing training for teaching staffs. When teachers are supported in their work with the tools they're likely to use, when training is grounded in pedagogy they're expected to deliver, and when they're allowed to provide feedback on what they've learned (or not learned) from training, they'll be far more capable of translating these techniques to their own classrooms or through remote learning opportunities. These are just good teaching practices, so why don't we use them to develop the people who actually teach our children?

A Closing Message

Although there's much work to be done, I'm optimistic about our future. The US has many of the finest schools and school districts in the world. We've set out on an ambitious and noble project: to educate all our children. Even during a global pandemic that has upended normal life, we've seen how our schools continue to be essential.

This doesn't mean we lack challenges. We're losing teachers and administrators at an increasing pace. Our adoption of technology lags behind that in other industries and sectors. Our students are experiencing anxiety, depression, loneliness, and other traumas at ever-increasing rates. But we need to celebrate our efforts and look to those innovative educators and schools that are paving the way into the future.

Yes, change is hard. But we have to be serious about facing it if we want to support our students.

Keep in mind: it's about evolution, not revolution—even in these unusual times. It's tempting to get stuck in the present moment, to deal with the latest calamity. But we need to keep our eyes on the future. We need to keep thinking about 2025 or 2030, not just today. Schools and educators must be future focused as we make instructional plans and incorporate new technologies. This means preparing our students for the world that's coming by giving them the skills they'll need to succeed in an augmented, automated workplace. If we want to maintain the strength of our economy, we need independent, creative doers and thinkers in our workforce.

I'm confident we can get there—we can make the needed changes—guided by thoughtful leaders who drive the evolution of education. As we assert our leadership, we'll see amazing improvements. I know it's comforting to return to what's familiar, but now is our chance to embrace a new normal. We need to seize this opportunity and implement broad changes that will help bring our school system into the twenty-first century. The future of our children depends on it.

LESSONS FOR THE FUTURE

- We've reached a tipping point in education. Being forced to rapidly switch to online learning as a result of COVID-19 has highlighted many of the strengths and weaknesses of technology, including issues with equity and SEL.
- The well-being of ALL students should be our top priority. Schools and educators need to shift the focus from content to the development of the whole child. We must be able to help students cope with new and existing stressors and address their needs through more individualized learning, community schools, and data-driven technology.

- Classrooms of the future will be blended. Supporting proven learning strategies with new digital tools will allow for greater customization of the learning process. It will also enable teachers to do what they do best—strengthen relationships, encourage individuals, and support the development of social and emotional skills.
- Teachers will continue to be essential, but the role of the teacher needs to evolve. Educators must improve their skills at managing the learning process, building relationships with their students and peers, and embracing technology in the classroom.
- As the role of the teacher changes, we need to recognize the additional burdens teachers face and do a better job of supporting them. Our professional learning plans should include resiliency training to help with emotional labor, and improved technology training to help with implementation. We should also do a better job of modeling the techniques and technologies we want to see in the classroom.
- Even with these challenges, I'm confident that together we'll succeed in helping ALL children thrive in the future!

Notes

Preface: The New Normal

1. Daggett, W. R. (2020, April). Re-entry and beyond: COVID-19 implications and considerations for K–12 school districts. International Center for Leadership in Education. Retrieved from https://leadered.com/resources/re-entry-and-beyond-covid-19-implications-and-considerations-for-k-12-school-districts/

Introduction

1. Employers rate career competencies, new hire proficiencies. (2017, December 11). National Association of Colleges and Employers. Retrieved from https://www.naceweb.org/career-readiness/competencies/employers-rate-career-competencies-new-hire-proficiency/
2. Petrone, P. (2019, January 1). The skills companies need most in 2019—and how to learn them [Web log post]. *Learning Blog*, LinkedIn. Retrieved from https://learning.linkedin.com/blog/top-skills/the-skills-companies-need-most-in-2019--and-how-to-learn-them
3. World Economic Forum. (2016, January). *The future of jobs: Employment, skills and workforce strategy for the fourth industrial revolution* [Executive summary]. Retrieved from http://www3.weforum.org/docs/WEF_FOJ_Executive_Summary_Jobs.pdf
4. Fry, R. (2017, May 5). It's becoming more common for young adults to live at home—and for longer stretches. Pew Research Center. Retrieved from https://www.pewresearch.org/fact-tank/2017/05/05/its-becoming-more-common-for-young-adults-to-live-at-home-and-for-longer-stretches/
5. Smith, K. A. (2019, April 24). Half of parents financially helping their adult children say it's putting retirement savings at risk. Bankrate. Retrieved from https://www.bankrate.com/personal-finance/financial-independence-survey-april-2019/

Chapter 1: Kids Today

1. Curtin, S. C., & Heron, M. P. (2019). Death rates due to suicide and homicide among persons aged 10–24: United States, 2000–2017. Retrieved

from https://stacks.cdc.gov/view/cdc/81944; Perou, R., Bitsko, R. H., Blumberg, S. J., Pastor, P., Ghandour, R. M., Gfroerer, J. C., & Huang, L. N. (2013). Mental health surveillance among children—United States, 2005–2011. *MMWR Supplement, 62*(2), 1–35.

2. World Health Organization. (2017). *Depression and other common mental disorders: Global health estimates* (No. WHO/MSD/MER/2017.2). Geneva, Switzerland: Author. Retrieved from https://www.who.int/mental_health/management/depression/prevalence_global_health_estimates/en/
3. Centers for Disease Control. (2015). Suicide: Facts at a glance. Retrieved from https://www.cdc.gov/violenceprevention/pdf/suicide-datasheet-a.pdf; Heron, M. (2019, June 24). Deaths: Leading causes for 2017. *National Vital Statistics Reports, 68*(6), 1–76.
4. National Institute of Mental Health. (2017, November). Prevalence of any anxiety disorder among adolescents. Retrieved from https://www.nimh.nih.gov/health/statistics/any-anxiety-disorder.shtml; Denizet-Lewis, B. (2017, October 11). Why are more American teenagers than ever suffering from severe anxiety? *New York Times Magazine.* Retrieved from https://www.nytimes.com/2017/10/11/magazine/why-are-more-american-teenagers-than-ever-suffering-from-severe-anxiety.html; Horowitz, J. M., & Graf, N. (2019, February 20). Most U.S. teens see anxiety and depression as a major problem among their peers. Pew Research Center. Retrieved from https://www.pewsocialtrends.org/2019/02/20/most-u-s-teens-see-anxiety-and-depression-as-a-major-problem-among-their-peers/
5. Dick, B., & Ferguson, B. J. (2015). Health for the world's adolescents: A second chance in the second decade. *Journal of Adolescent Health, 56*(1), 3–6; Blue Cross Blue Shield. (2018). *Major depression: The impact on overall health.* Retrieved from https://www.bcbs.com/sites/default/files/file-attachments/health-of-america-report/HoA_Major_Depression_Report.pdf; Geiger, A. W., & Davis, L. (2019, July 12). A growing number of American teenagers—particularly girls—are facing depression. Pew Research Center. Retrieved from https://www.pewresearch.org/fact-tank/2019/07/12/a-growing-number-of-american-teenagers-particularly-girls-are-facing-depression/
6. Connelly, S. (2014). *Looking further with Ford 2020 trends.* Retrieved from https://media.ford.com/content/dam/fordmedia/North%20America/US/2019/12/11/2020-Ford-Trends.pdf; Twenge, J. M. (2017, September). Have smartphones destroyed a generation? *Atlantic, 9.* Retrieved from https://www.theatlantic.com/magazine/archive/2017/09/has-the-smartphone-destroyed-a-generation/534198/
7. Valtorta, N. K., Kanaan, M., Gilbody, S., Ronzi, S., & Hanratty, B. (2016). Loneliness and social isolation as risk factors for coronary heart disease and stroke: Systematic review and meta-analysis of longitudinal observational studies. *Heart, 102,* 1009–1016; Manning-Schaffel, V. (2018, May 14). Americans

are lonelier than ever—but 'Gen Z' may be the loneliest. *Better* (NBC News). Retrieved from https://www.nbcnews.com/better/pop-culture/americans-are-lonelier-ever-gen-z-may-be-loneliest-ncna873101

8. CollegeBoard. (2016). SAT suite results overview. Retrieved from https://reports.collegeboard.org/archive/sat-suite-program-results/2016/overview
9. Karlgaard, R. (2019). *Late bloomers: The power of patience in a world obsessed with early achievement* (p. 29). New York, NY: Currency.
10. Wooten, C. (2018, August 7). Surviving myself. *New York Times.* Retrieved from https://www.nytimes.com/2018/08/07/opinion/self-harm-cutting-teenagers.html; Baumgaertner, E. (2018, July 2). How many teenage girls deliberately harm themselves? Nearly 1 in 4, survey finds. *New York Times.* Retrieved from https://www.nytimes.com/2018/07/02/health/self-harm-teenagers-cdc.html; Monto, M. A., McRee, N., & Deryck, F. S. (2018). Nonsuicidal self-injury among a representative sample of US adolescents, 2015. *American Journal of Public Health, 108,* 1042–1048.
11. Anxiety and Depression Association of America. (2015). Children and teens. Retrieved from https://adaa.org/living-with-anxiety/children
12. Twenge, Have smartphones destroyed a generation?
13. Krishnan, S. S., & Sitaraman, R. K. (2013). Video stream quality impacts viewer behavior: Inferring causality using quasi-experimental designs. *IEEE/ACM Transactions on Networking, 21,* 2001–2014.
14. Anderson, M. (2018). A majority of teens have experienced some form of cyberbullying. Pew Research Center. Retrieved from https://www.pewresearch.org/internet/2018/09/27/a-majority-of-teens-have-experienced-some-form-of-cyberbullying/
15. Lenhart, A. (2015, August 6). Chapter 5: Conflict, friendships and technology. *Pew Research Center: Internet, Science & Tech.* Retrieved from https://www.pewresearch.org/internet/2015/08/06/chapter-5-conflict-friendships-and-technology/
16. Ross, C. C. (2012, August 13). Overexposed and under-prepared: The effects of early exposure to sexual content [Web log post]. *Psychology Today.* Retrieved from https://www.psychologytoday.com/us/blog/real-healing/201208/overexposed-and-under-prepared-the-effects-early-exposure-sexual-content
17. Wergin, C. (2015, March 15). The case for free-range parenting. *New York Times.* Retrieved from https://www.nytimes.com/2015/03/20/opinion/the-case-for-free-range-parenting.html; Larson, L. R., Green, G. T., & Cordell, H. K. (2011). Children's time outdoors: Results and implications of the National Kids Survey. *Journal of Park and Recreation Administration 29*(2), 1–20.
18. Sentencing Project. (2016, February 1). Incarcerated women and girls. Retrieved from https://www.sentencingproject.org/wp-content/

uploads/2016/02/Incarcerated-Women-and-Girls.pdf; Noel, M., & Najowski, C. (2019, September 1). When parents are incarcerated, their children are punished, too. *Monitor on Psychology, 50*(8). Retrieved from https://www.apa.org/monitor/2019/09/jn; Murphey, D., & Cooper, P. M. (2015, October). *Parents behind bars: What happens to their children?* Child Trends. Retrieved from https://www.childtrends.org/publications/parents-behind-bars-what-happens-to-their-children; Jackson, D. B., & Vaughn, M. G. (2017). Parental incarceration and child sleep and eating behaviors. *Journal of Pediatrics, 185*, 211–217; Gifford, E. J., Kozecke, L. E., Golonka, M., Hill, S. N., Costello, E. J., Shanahan, L., & Copeland, W. E. (2019). Association of parental incarceration with psychiatric and functional outcomes of young adults. *JAMA Network Open, 2*(8), e1910005. Retrieved from https://doi.org/10.1001/jamanetworkopen.2019.10005

19. Edwards, E. J. (2019). Helping the unseen: Providing educational equity for students experiencing homelessness. In T. C. Howard (Ed.), *All students must thrive: Transforming schools to combat toxic stressors and cultivate critical wellness* (pp. 148–170). Boston, MA: Houghton Mifflin Harcourt.
20. Ibid.
21. Howard, M. (2019). How to create a trauma-aware learning environment. In T. C. Howard (Ed.), *All students must thrive: Transforming schools to combat toxic stressors and cultivate critical wellness* (pp. 19–44). Boston, MA: Houghton Mifflin Harcourt.
22. Twenge, J. M., Zhang, L., & Im, C. (2004). It's beyond my control: A cross-temporal meta-analysis of increasing externality in locus of control, 1960–2002. *Personality and Social Psychology Review, 8*, 308–319; Pryor, J. H., Hurtado, S., DeAngelo, L. E., Blake, L. P., & Tran, S. (2010). *The American freshman: National norms fall 2009.* Berkeley: University of California Press.
23. Howard, T. (2019). Developing racial literacy and cultural awareness in schools and classrooms. In T. C. Howard (Ed.), *All students must thrive: Transforming schools to combat toxic stressors and cultivate critical wellness* (pp. 2–3). Boston, MA: Houghton Mifflin Harcourt.
24. Ibid.
25. Cai, W., & Patel, J. K. (2019, May 11). A half-century of school shootings like Columbine, Sandy Hook and Parkland. *New York Times*. Retrieved from https://www.nytimes.com/interactive/2019/05/11/us/school-shootings-united-states.html
26. Smith, M., & Lu, D. (2020, January 6). An overlooked danger: School shootings after hours. *New York Times.* Retrieved from https://www.nytimes.com/interactive/2020/01/06/us/after-school-shootings.html?action=click&module=Top%20Stories&pgtype=Homepage

Chapter 2: Their Future World

1. Pelly, S. (2019, August 4). Making ideas into reality at MIT's "future factory." *60 Minutes*. Retrieved from https://www.cbsnews.com/news/60-minutes-mit-media-lab-making-ideas-into-reality-future-factory-2019-08-04/
2. Susskind, D. (2020). *A world without work: Technology, automation, and how we should respond*. New York, NY: Metropolitan Books; Vincent, J. (2018, August 13). DeepMind's AI can detect over 50 eye diseases as accurately as a doctor. *Verge*. Retrieved from https://www.theverge.com/2018/8/13/17670156/deepmind-ai-eye-disease-doctor-moorfields; Hollon, T. C., Pandian, B., Adapa, A. R., Urias, E., Save, A. V., Khalsa, S.S.S., . . . Petridis, P. D. (2020, January 6). Near real-time intraoperative brain tumor diagnosis using stimulated Raman histology and deep neural networks. *Nature Medicine*, *26*, 52–58. Retrieved from https://doi.org/10.1038/s41591-019-0715-9; Mozur, P. (2017, May 23). Google's AlphaGo defeats Chinese Go master in win for AI. *New York Times*. Retrieved from https://www.nytimes.com/2017/05/23/business/google-deepmind-alphago-go-champion-defeat.html; Metz, C. (2019, May 30). DeepMind can now beat us at multiplayer games, too. *New York Times*. Retrieved from https://www.nytimes.com/2019/05/30/science/deep-mind-artificial-intelligence.html
3. Summers, L. (2016, September 26). Men without work. RSS Archive. Retrieved from http://larrysummers.com/2016/09/26/men-without-work/
4. Barrero, J. M., Bloom, N., & Davis, S. J. (2020). COVID-19 is also a reallocation shock (No. w27137). National Bureau of Economic Research. Retrieved from https://bfi.uchicago.edu/working-paper/covid-19-is-also-a-reallocation-shock/
5. Craver, J. (2015, July 27). Companies focusing less on traditional benefits. BenefitsPRO.com. Retrieved from http://www.benefitspro.com/2015/07/27/companies-focusing-less-on-traditional-benefits; Brandon, E. (2014, July 28). Workplace benefits that are disappearing. *U.S. News & World Report*. Retrieved from http://money.usnews.com/money/retirement/articles/2014/07/28/workplace-benefits-that-are-disappearing; Terhune, C. (2013, May 2). Part-timers to lose pay amid health act's new math. *Los Angeles Times*. Retrieved from http://articles.latimes.com/2013/may/02/business/la-fi-part-time-healthcare-20130502
6. Debter, L. (2019, May 15). Amazon surpasses Walmart as the world's largest retailer. *Forbes*. Retrieved from https://www.forbes. com/sites/laurendebter/2019/05/15/worlds-largest-retailers-2019-amazon-walmart-alibaba/#10ea6c5f4171
7. King, K. (2020, February 21). The robot in aisle five isn't stalking you. No, really. *Wall Street Journal*. Retrieved from https://www.wsj.com/articles/the-robot-in-aisle-five-isnt-stalking-you-no-really-11582302075

8. Hess, E. M. (2020). The ten largest employers in America. *USA Today.* Retrieved from https://www.usatoday.com/story/money/business/2013/08/22/ten-largest-employers/2680249/
9. Satterfield, D. (2015). There's never been a better time to invest in tech. Here's why. Rogue Economics. Retrieved from https://www.rogueeconomics.com/bill-bonner-diary/theres-never-been-a-better-time-to-invest-in-tech-heres-why/
10. TED. (2017, February 28). The incredible inventions of intuitive AI: Maurice Conti [Video file]. Retrieved from https://www.youtube.com/watch?v=aR5N2Jl8k14
11. Frey, C., & Osborne, M. (2013). *The future of employment: How susceptible are jobs to computerization?* Oxford, UK: University of Oxford. Retrieved from http://www.oxfordmartin.ox.ac.uk/downloads/academic/The_Future_of_Employment.pdf
12. US Census Bureau. (2011, January 7). Quick Facts. Retrieved from https://www.census.gov/quickfacts/table/PST045215/00
13. UBS. (2018). Think you know the next gen investor? Think again. *UBS Investor Watch.* Retrieved from https://www.ubs.com/us/en/investor-watch/2018/millennial-attitudes.html
14. Pew Research Center. (2014, March 7). Millennials in adulthood: Detached from institutions, networked with friends. Pew Research Center. Retrieved from https://www.pewsocialtrends.org/2014/03/07/millennials-in-adulthood/
15. Fry, R. (2017, May 5). It's becoming more common for young adults to live at home—and for longer stretches. Pew Research Center. Retrieved from https://www.pewresearch.org/fact-tank/2017/05/05/its-becoming-more-common-for-young-adults-to-live-at-home-and-for-longer-stretches/
16. Bureau of Labor Statistics. (2016). *Occupational outlook handbook, 2016–17 edition.* Retrieved from http://www.bls.gov/ooh/
17. Bughin, J., Hazan, E., Lund, S., Dahlström, P., Wiesinger, A., & Subramaniam, A. (2018, May 23). Skill shift: Automation and the future of the workforce. McKinsey Global Institute. Retrieved from https://www.mckinsey.com/featured-insights/future-of-work/skill-shift-automation-and-the-future-of-the-workforce
18. Career Readiness Partner Council. (2014). *Building blocks for change: What it means to be career ready.* Retrieved from http://www.ascd.org/publications/newsletters/policy-priorities/vol20/num03/The-Career-Readiness-Partner-Council.aspx
19. American Institutes for Research. (2012, September 18). Big gaps in earnings for Tennessee college grads [Press release]. Retrieved from http://www.air.org/news/press-release/big-gaps-earnings-tennessee-college-grads
20. Wagner, T., & Dintersmith, T. (2015). *Most likely to succeed: Preparing our kids for the innovation era.* New York, NY: Simon & Schuster.

21. Institute for the Future. (2017). The next era of human/machine partnerships: Emerging technologies' impact on society & work in 2030. Dell Technologies. Retrieved from https://www.delltechnologies.com/content/dam/delltechnologies/assets/perspectives/2030/pdf/SR1940_IFTFforDellTechnologies_Human-Machine_070517_readerhigh-res.pdf

Chapter 3: Developing the Whole Child

1. Durlak, J. A., Domitrovich, C. E., Weissberg, R. P., & Gullotta, T. P. (Eds.). (2015). *Handbook of social and emotional learning: Research and practice.* New York, NY: Guilford Press.
2. Immordino-Yang, M. H. (2015). *Emotions, learning, and the brain: Exploring the educational implications of affective neuroscience* (Norton Series on the Social Neuroscience of Education) (p. 18). New York, NY: Norton.
3. Ibid.
4. Carmangian, P. (2019). It's not so much . . . for a grade. In T. Howard (Ed.), *All students must thrive: Transforming schools to combat toxic stressors and cultivate critical wellness* (pp. 125–147). Boston, MA: Houghton Mifflin Harcourt.
5. Daggett, W. (2019). *The tipping point: Developing a strategic plan for addressing social/emotional learning systemwide.* Boston, MA: Houghton Mifflin Harcourt.
6. Bailey, R., Stickle, L., Brion-Meisels, G., & Jones, S. M. (2019). Reimagining social-emotional learning: Findings from a strategy-based approach. *Phi Delta Kappan, 100*(5), 53–58; Jones, S. M., & Kahn, J. (2017). The evidence base for how we learn: Supporting students' social, emotional, and academic development. Consensus statements of evidence from the Council of Distinguished Scientists. Aspen Institute. Retrieved from https://assets.aspeninstitute.org/content/uploads/2017/09/SEAD-Research-Brief-9.12_updated-web.pdf
7. Embry, D. D., & Biglan, A. (2008). Evidence-based kernels: Fundamental units of behavioral influence. *Clinical Child and Family Psychology Review, 11*(3), 75–113. Retrieved from https://link.springer.com/article/10.1007/s10567-008-0036-x

Chapter 4: Rigor and Relevance: It Now Starts with Relationships

1. Daggett, W., & Jones, S. (2019). *Addressing whole child growth through strong relationships: The evidence-based connections between academic and social-emotional learning.* Boston, MA: Houghton Mifflin Harcourt.
2. Umberson, D., & Karas Montez, J. (2010). Social relationships and health: A flashpoint for health policy. *Journal of Health and Social Behavior, 51*(1 Suppl.), S54–S66.

3. Bandura, A. (1993). Perceived self-efficacy in cognitive development and functioning. *Educational Psychologist, 28*, 117–148; Bandura, A. (1982). Self-efficacy mechanism in human agency. *American Psychologist, 37*, 122; Zimmerman, B. J. (2000). Self-efficacy: An essential motive to learn. *Contemporary Educational Psychology, 25*(1), 82–91; Stajkovic, A. D., & Luthans, F. (1998). Social cognitive theory and self-efficacy: Going beyond traditional motivational and behavioral approaches. *Organizational Dynamics, 26*(4), 62–75; Schunk, D. H. (1991). Self-efficacy and academic motivation. *Educational Psychologist, 26*, 207–231; Gist, M. E., & Mitchell, T. R. (1992). Self-efficacy: A theoretical analysis of its determinants and malleability. *Academy of Management Review, 17*, 183–211; Pajares, F. (1996). Self-efficacy beliefs in academic settings. *Review of Educational Research, 66*, 543–578; Ajzen, I. (2002). Perceived behavioral control, self-efficacy, locus of control, and the theory of planned behavior 1. *Journal of Applied Social Psychology, 32*, 665–683; Multon, K. D., Brown, S. D., & Lent, R. W. (1991). Relation of self-efficacy beliefs to academic outcomes: A meta-analytic investigation. *Journal of Counseling Psychology, 38*(1), 30; Zimmerman, B. J., Bandura, A., & Martinez-Pons, M. (1992). Self-motivation for academic attainment: The role of self-efficacy beliefs and personal goal setting. *American Educational Research Journal, 29*, 663–676; Stajkovic, A. D., & Luthans, F. (1998). Self-efficacy and work-related performance: A meta-analysis. *Psychological Bulletin, 124*, 240–261; Schwarzer, R. (Ed.). (2014). *Self-efficacy: Thought control of action*. New York, NY: Routledge; Weiss, M. R., Wiese, D. M., & Klint, K. A. (1989). Head over heels with success: The relationship between self-efficacy and performance in competitive youth gymnastics. *Journal of Sport & Exercise Psychology, 11*, 444–451.
4. Ramachandran, V. S. (2012). *Encyclopedia of human behavior*. Cambridge, MA: Academic Press.
5. Hattie, J., & Zierer, K. (2017). *10 mindframes for visible learning: Teaching for success*. New York, NY: Routledge.
6. Cheung, C.S.S., & Pomerantz, E. M. (2012). Why does parents' involvement enhance children's achievement? The role of parent-oriented motivation. *Journal of Educational Psychology, 104*, 820–832; Pomerantz, E. M., Kim, E. M., & Cheung, C.S.S. (2012). Parents' involvement in children's learning. In K. R. Harris, S. Graham, T. Urdan, S. Graham, J. M. Royer, & M. Zeidner (Eds.), *APA educational psychology handbook*, Vol. 2. Individual differences and cultural and contextual factors (pp. 417–440). Washington, DC: American Psychological Association; Wang, M. T., & Sheikh-Khalil, S. (2014). Does parental involvement matter for student achievement and mental health in high school? *Child Development, 85*, 610–625.

Chapter 5: Future Focused, Not Forward Focused

1. Sarason, S. B. (1996). *Revisiting the culture of the school and the problem of change.* New York, NY: Teachers College Press.
2. Kagan, J. (2020, January 23). Zero-based budgeting (ZBB). *Investopedia.* Retrieved from https://www.investopedia.com/terms/z/zbb.asp

Chapter 6: Growth over Proficiency

1. How did U.S. students perform on the most recent assessments? (2020). Nation's Report Card. Retrieved from https://www.nationsreportcard.gov
2. Rose, T. (2017). *The end of average: Unlocking our potential by embracing what makes us different* (p. 84). San Francisco, CA: HarperOne.
3. Ibid., p. 91.
4. Weber, J. (2015, July 2). What employers really want from millennials. Talent Management & HR. Retrieved from https://www.tlnt.com/what-employers-really-want-from-millennials/

Chapter 7: Data: The Driver of School and District Decisions

1. Katie Lyon and Tom Matson of Gallup Education, interview with the author, January 14, 2020.

Chapter 8: The Classroom of the Future

1. UNESCO. (2020). Education: From disruption to discovery. Retrieved from https://en.unesco.org/covid19/educationresponse; Map: Coronavirus and school closures. (2020, May 15). *Education Week.* Retrieved from https://www.edweek.org/ew/section/multimedia/map-coronavirus-and-school-closures.html
2. Editorial Board. (2020, April 16). 50 million kids can't attend school. What happens to them? *New York Times.* Retrieved from https://www.nytimes.com/2020/04/16/opinion/coronavirus-schools-closed.html; Editorial Board. (2020, March 27). Locked out of the virtual classroom. *New York Times.* Retrieved from https://www.nytimes.com/2020/03/27/opinion/coronavirus-internet-schools-learning.html; Edwards, E. J. (2019). Helping the unseen: Providing educational equity for students experiencing homelessness. In T. C. Howard (Ed.), *All students must thrive: Transforming schools to combat toxic stressors and cultivate critical wellness* (pp. 148–170). Boston, MA: Houghton Mifflin Harcourt.
3. Goldstein, D., Popescu, A., & Hannah-Jones, N. (2020, April 6). As school moves online, many students stay logged out. *New York Times.* Retrieved

from https://www.nytimes.com/2020/04/06/us/coronavirus-schools-attendance-absent.html

4. This is an often quoted, but paraphrased, comment by Mahatma Gandhi. What he actually said is as follows: "We but mirror the world. All the tendencies present in the outer world are to be found in the world of our body. If we could change ourselves, the tendencies in the world would also change. As a man changes his own nature, so does the attitude of the world change towards him. This is the divine mystery supreme. A wonderful thing it is and the source of our happiness. We need not wait to see what others do."
5. Daggett, W. (2020, April). Re-entry and beyond: COVID-19 implications and considerations for K–12 school districts. International Center for Leadership in Education. Retrieved from https://leadered.com/resources/re-entry-and-beyond-covid-19-implications-and-considerations-for-k-12-school-districts/
6. Kieschnick, W. (2017). *Bold school: Old school wisdom + new school technologies = blended learning that works.* Boston, MA: Houghton Mifflin Harcourt.
7. Ibid,. p. 9.
8. Kaplan, E. (2019, July 19). Teaching your heart out: Emotional labor and the need for systemic change. *Edutopia.* Retrieved from https://www.edutopia.org/article/teaching-your-heart-out-emotional-labor-and-need-systemic-change

4500913409-0607-2025
Printed in the U.S.A